Handle With Care

The Emotional Intelligence Activity Book

6seconds

Emotional Intelligence Activity Book

Second Edition, Revised and Updated ©2001, 1997/1998
Joshua M. Freedman, Anabel L. Jensen, Ph.D.,
Marsha C. Rideout, Patricia E. Freedman
Photocollages copyright © 1997/1998, Joshua Freedman

Published by Six Seconds
a nonprofit educational service organization supporting emotional intelligence
for families, schools, communities, and corporations.
316 Seville Way, San Mateo, California, 94402

Library of Congress Catalog Number: LCN
ISBN 0-9629123-2-8

Multiple copies of books and materials from Six Seconds are available at a
discount for educational use.
Please contact the publisher at (650) 685-9885.

Acknowledgments

We would like to thank Karen and George McCown for their deep commitment to making this work possible. It is an exceptional privilege to work in an organization where we can spend our days promoting our noble goals and shared vision.

This Second Edition was published with support from the Laursen Family Foundation; we are grateful for their generous support. Thanks also to: Shanna Swan, Grace Jordan, and Deborah Lustig for use of photos. To Judith Barnes of Lindentree books for book inspiration.

Since the publication of the first edition, we have received appreciations and feedback from all over the world. It has been my great pleasure to interact with and learn from so many EQ advocates. Most of all, thank you to Patty, I do not know how I could create without your love and support — our work is a reflection of our relationship. The sun rises in your eyes.

— Josh

Thank you to my family — immediate, extended, and honorary members — for gracing my life with so many gifts. And to my son, Caleb, who has taught me so much.

— Anabel

My gratitude and love to all the children in my life, especially Bryan, Eric, Mary Heather, and Katie, who have expanded the spectrum of my emotions. And to my father who was my model of creativity and integrity.

— Marsha

Emotional
Intelligence
Courage
Adversity
Perseverance
Interdependenc
Empathy
Creativity
Noble Goal
Motivation
Curiosity
Accountability
Optimism
Forgiveness
Initiative
Conflict
Humor
Tolerance
Service
Truth
Tranquility
Awareness
Resiliency
Self-Control
Fusion
Integrity

Take six seconds to visit us on the internet!

www.6seconds.org/hwc

Contents

Emotional
Intelligence
Courage

Adversity

Perseverance

Interdependence

Empathy

Creativity

Noble Goal

Motivation

Curiosity

Accountability

Optimism

Forgiveness

Initiative

Conflict

H u m o r

Tolerance

Service

Truth

Tranquility

Awareness

Resiliency

Self-Control

Fusion

Integrity

This chart will help you find your way around *Handle With Care*. Across the top are frequently occurring issues and needs. If you are looking for resources for one of these, look down the chart to see which of the 24 themes are marked with a ● as a fruitful starting point.

Themes / Frequent Issues and Needs	Grief	Exclusion	Depression	Energy	Anger	Fear	Relationships	Self-awareness	Self-management	Self-direction	Loneliness	Decision Making
Courage				●		●					●	●
Adversity	●		●							●		
Perseverance				●					●			
Interdependence			●				●				●	●
Empathy	●	●	●		●		●					●
Creativity			●					●				●
Noble Goal	●		●	●						●		
Motivation			●							●		●
Curiosity					●	●		●				
Accountability			●							●		●
Optimism	●		●	●						●	●	
Forgiveness		●	●		●		●			●		
Initiative			●								●	●
Conflict					●		●					
Humor			●	●								
Tolerance		●					●	●				
Service	●		●								●	●
Truth		●				●			●			
Tranquility	●		●						●			
Awareness							●	●				●
Resiliency	●		●	●						●		
Self-Control					●				●			
Fusion			●						●			●
Integrity								●	●	●		●

RESULTS OF EQ

As EQ is learned, it leads to an increase in certain interpersonal and intra-personal behaviors. As you consider learning and teaching EQ, it is important to identify behaviors that will result from the learning. Some of the actions that reflect increasing EQ are:

- Talking about feelings and needs
- Listening, sharing, comforting
- Growing from conflict and adversity
- Prioritizing and then setting goals
- Including others
- Making conscious decisions
- Anticipating consequences
- Giving time and resources to the larger community
- Facilitating effective communication
- Taking positive risks
- Asking high-order questions

These behaviors develop:

- Stronger persistence
- Increased optimism
- Improved problem solving abilities
- Heightened creativity and curiosity
- Greater cooperation
- Intensified trustworthiness and dependability
- Continued commitment to learning and growth

Emotional Intelligence

Courage

Adversity

Perseverance

Interdependence

Empathy

Creativity

Noble Goal

Motivation

Curiosity

Accountability

Optimism

Forgiveness

Initiative

Conflict

Humor

Tolerance

Service

Truth

Tranquility

Awareness

Resiliency

Self-Control

Fusion

Integrity

How To Use This Book

The *Handle With Care Activity Book* is an open-ended tool for promoting emotional intelligence. The book is an invitation to ponder, to experiment, and to grow. Each of the 24 themes includes:

- An explanation of the theme.
- Activities for individuals, families, classrooms, or groups.
- Inspiring quotes, role models, books, and movies to help you expand your understanding and see applications of the theme.
- Questions about each theme to promote thoughtful reflection.
- Photo collage illustrations to invite a further contemplation.

In addition, this book includes over 150 stickers and 12 postcards (in the back). These are to encourage you to practice EQ skills, to celebrate growth, and to reach out to others.

Use the book in any order. Pick activities at random, or systematically focus on one theme at a time. This is a resource book, keep it handy and turn to it on a regular basis. There is no "right" approach – except, as with any skill, if you want to learn EQ, you need to persevere.

On the internet at **www.6seconds.org**, the publisher is collecting ideas for using this book. Visit, look for ideas, and share yours. The effect of increased emotional intelligence is multiplied when it is a group effort: together we are better. Six Seconds encourages you to join its network of people committed to the power of emotional intelligence to make an improved tomorrow.

Books and Movies

Books and movies are listed for each theme. They are divided into resources for "younger people" and "older people"; while "older people" resources are intended for middle school and beyond, the authors suggest that teachers and parents read/view any resources before sharing them with children.

If you can not find the books in your local bookstore or library, most are listed at **www.6seconds.org/hwc** with information and links to order them online.

Handle With Care at Home

Here are some suggestions for using this book at home:

- Have EQ family dinners where you talk about and experiment with one theme for the evening.
- Have an EQ party with friends and neighbors.

- Put the stickers on the family calendar or someplace prominent. Use them to celebrate EQ accomplishments.
- Keep a copy of the book in the car, and discuss questions while car-pooling and on road trips.
- While reading or watching television, discuss the characters, their behavior patterns, and other options for solutions.
- Keep a journal of your own ideas/thoughts/techniques/etc. for increasing your level of emotional awareness and for documenting your progress.

HANDLE WITH CARE AT SCHOOL

- Pick an EQ theme for your class or school for the month, or even the year. Send activity ideas home, invite students to try asking the fusion questions of their parents, or have an all school celebration of the theme.
- Use the quotes as a "warm-up" activity each morning — write one on the board, have students copy it into their journals, and then have them draw pictures or write about the meaning of the quote. Follow the warm-up with a brief discussion.
- Ask students to keep track of examples of the themes in their daily lives. Before recess or during transitions, ask them to share these stories.
- Look for themes in books, and discuss how characters do and do not demonstrate EQ.
- Invite a younger or older "buddy-class" to try some of the activities with yours. Put students in small, multi-age groups and let them choose from several activities.
- Make your own postcards, or order more from Six Seconds, and use them in language arts.

HANDLE WITH CARE IN ORGANIZATIONS

- Start team meetings with a brief EQ activity from the book.
- Ask team members to share examples of their colleagues' "high EQ behaviors" and other appreciations, and email a list to the entire company once a month.
- Invite colleagues to participate in a monthly EQ Lunch where you discuss the book, try activities, and share how participants have been using the activities at home.
- Use the stickers on your team planning calendar to acknowledge positive EQ progress.
- Integrate EQ goal-setting in annual reviews; have all team members pick a theme to develop for themselves, including specific, measurable objectives, such as, "practice one activity from the book each month."

Emotional
Intelligence

Courage

Adversity

Perseverance

Interdependence

Empathy

Creativity

Noble Goal

Motivation

Curiosity

Accountability

Optimism

Forgiveness

Initiative

Conflict

Humor

Tolerance

Service

Truth

Tranquility

Awareness

Resiliency

Self-Control

Fusion

Integrity

HANDLE WITH CARE IN ORGANIZATIONS *CONTINUED*

- Each Monday, write one of the quotes on an elegant card and give it to a colleague as a thank you gift for something s/he did or said the previous week. Be sure to say why you are giving this particular quote.
- When travelling, email back and forth with your family about one theme, question, or activity. If you are travelling with colleagues, all of you pick the same theme so you can extend the dialogue.
- Invite personnel to join an EQ task force which will select one theme per quarter and work together to raise awareness.

SIX SECONDS OF EMOTIONAL INTELLIGENCE

Our model for learning and teaching EQ is "Know Yourself," "Choose Yourself," and "Give Yourself."

Know Yourself is increasing self-awareness. It is based on understanding how you function.

Choose Yourself is building self-management. It focuses on consciously directing your thoughts, feelings, and actions.

Give Yourself is using self-direction. It has to do with using emotional intelligence to take your place in the larger world.

We have identified eight key skills, or fundamentals, of emotional intelligence. They are divided into the three parts of the model. Like all kinds of intelligence, there are developmental aspects to this learning (as we get older, our abilities become more sophisticated and complex) and our ability to use this intelligence varies situation to situation, day to day.

EQ FUNDAMENTALS :

1. Build Emotional Literacy
2. Recognize Patterns
3. Apply Consequential Thinking
4. Evaluate and Re-choose
5. Engage Intrinsic Motivation
6. Choose Optimism
7. Create Empathy
8. Commit to Noble Goals

KNOW YOURSELF:

BUILD EMOTIONAL LITERACY

Feelings are a complex aspect of every person. While research has identified eight "core" feelings (fear, joy, acceptance, anger, sorrow, disgust, surprise, expectation), we each experience dozens, even hundreds, of variations each day. These emotions blend and merge, and frequently they conflict. This EQ fundamental helps us sort out all of those feelings, name them, and begin to understand their causes and effects. It also helps us understand how emotions function in our brains & bodies, and the interaction of thought, feeling, and action, plus the recognition that we feel/experience multiple emotions simultaneously.

RECOGNIZE PATTERNS

The human brain follows patterns, or neural pathways. Stimulus leads to response, and over time, the response becomes nearly automatic. The pathway becomes a road, the road a highway, and the highway a super expressway - until it requires extraordinary measures to interrupt the automatic process.

The patterns of thinking lead to patterns of behavior. At a young age, we learn lessons of how to cope, how to get our needs met, how to protect ourselves. These strategies reinforce one another, and we develop a complex structure of beliefs to support the validity of the behaviors.

As we become more conscious of the patterns we exhibit, it becomes possible to: 1) analyze the beliefs and replace them if appropriate, and 2) interrupt the pattern and replace it with conscious behavior that moves us closer to our real goals. This is an enormously difficult task that requires commitment and vigilance - but it is not difficult to begin. It can be as simple as a six second pause to allow the conscious brain to begin to intervene in the pattern.

CHOOSE YOURSELF:

APPLY CONSEQUENTIAL THINKING

People are often told to control their emotions, to suppress feelings like anger, joy, or fear, and cut them off from the decision-making process. This old paradigm suggests that emotions make us less effective; nothing could be farther from reality. Feelings provide insight, energy, and are the real basis for almost every decision. Instead of disconnecting our emotions, we need to control our actions so that we have time to make the most creative, insight-ful, and powerful decisions. Particularly when dealing with conflict or crisis, we need to slow down the process and apply carefully practiced strategies that lead to decisions informed by the fused powers of heart and mind.

This "habit of mind" stems from a clear understanding of the consequences of our choices and the ability to imagine the cause and effect relationships. This process allows us to be as impulsive as we truly want to be - but it also allows us to limit impulsivity when the consequences are undesirable.

Emotional Intelligence

Courage

Adversity

Perseverance

Interdependence

Empathy

Creativity

Noble Goal

Motivation

Curiosity

Accountability

Optimism

Forgiveness

Initiative

Conflict

Humor

Tolerance

Service

Truth

Tranquility

Awareness

Resiliency

Self-Control

Fusion

Integrity

One key mechanism to develop and monitor consequential thinking is "self-talk." Self-talk is a mechanism to mentally explore multiple options and viewpoints; it provides a system to balance the various aspects of our self. Just as in conversations outside ourselves, sometimes the louder voice gets more attention; the challenge is to develop a process where listening is valued and all the voices - loud or soft - are heard.

EVALUATE AND RE-CHOOSE

In our daily lives, we have countless opportunities to get feedback about our thoughts, feelings, and actions, and to then change if the feedback so warrants. Unfortunately, we also have a great capacity to ignore this feed-back and blithely continue with a scarcity of useful information. In this unconscious state it is easy to become selfish, to sever connections with our humanity, and to subjugate ourselves to addictions or other compensations.

The alternative is to listen - to listen to ourselves, to listen to others. When we become skilled at sensing our own emotions, we are able to tap into the energy that they provide and take action. Emotions are energy – the challenge is to refine and utilize that energy – to carefully choose how we will use that power. Evaluating and re-choosing is simply a process of more consciously directing our thoughts, feelings, and actions.

ENGAGE INTRINSIC MOTIVATION

"Motivation" comes from Latin "to move." In essence, we take action because it feels good to do so. The challenge is to make it feel right to take action that does not have an immediate reward. To do so, we've got to tap into the part of ourselves that has a longer-view; which leads us to feel good about taking action even if there is not an immediate reward. We each make countless decisions each hour. What should I eat for lunch? What clothes should I wear today? Which book should I read? Which person should I ask? In part, we make those decisions unconsciously based on our patterns and habits. In part, we make those decisions based on our personal priorities. So, if we want to redirect our decision to take a longer-term view, we need to both shape unconscious habits and examine priorities to make sure they match.

In addition to motivating ourselves, it is important to learn how to motivate others. There are many ways to do so; the most obvious are "extrinsic" motivations. For example, "If you carry my bag, I'll give you a candy bar," is a simple example of extrinsic motivation - it is a bribe or a type of commer-cial interaction. Quite useful at times - but it doesn't last; the rewards have to get bigger and bigger, and you teach "obedience" rather than initiative. Building lasting motivation requires a more complex strategy; one based primarily on intrinsic motivation. Building motivation in others begins with three elements:

1. They need to feel the benefit of the priority you are suggesting. If you want a child to use a more polite vocabulary, s/he needs to experience how such a decision would feel good. S/he will develop that experience by being spoken to with polite words - at the same time, it might feel good to avoid the consequences of using impolite words - and that will feel good.

2. Treat them as you want them to be. As a child, Josh's mother always treated him as if he were honest - even when he wasn't. He internalized that value and struggled to improve his actions because it felt good to have his real behavior meet that high standard.

3. Give time. Motivation is a complex process and a vital one. Like so many intrapersonal skills, it often takes years or decades for the seeds to bloom.

Finally, it might be useful to recall some "anti-motivators." These include: lack of choice/control, repetitive tasks, inadequate feedback, and sarcasm.

CHOOSE OPTIMISM

Children are born optimistic, and tend to stay optimistic until they are six or seven. At that time, life's difficulties impinge enough that the door is opened for hopelessness. Research suggests that to avoid getting trapped in the negativity, people need at least one refuge. The refuge can be a person or a practice (such as reading) that provides positive input. It is remarkable to think that one source of kindness, one source of comfort, one source of hope is enough to combat the terrible perils that some children experience. Oprah Winfrey, for example, found refuge from abuse in books - and grew to become a powerfully optimistic adult.

Optimism validates our long-term motivation because it lets us see the future as positive and worthwhile. Optimism allows us to see beyond the present and feel good about what may happen. It is closely tied to resiliency and to perseverance, which are two skills that most affect our ability to function despite the difficulties of day-to-day life. Ayman Sawaf, Founder of the Foundation for Education in Emotional Literacy, says, "the future creates the present." It is not the past which creates the present, but a projection of the future which creates today.

Optimists see positive experiences as permanent, personal, and pervasive. If

Emotional Intelligence

Courage

Adversity

Perseverance

Interdependence

Empathy

Creativity

Noble Goal

Motivation

Curiosity

Accountability

Optimism

Forgiveness

Initiative

Conflict

Humor

Tolerance

Service

Truth

Tranquility

Awareness

Resiliency

Self-Control

Fusion

Integrity

an optimist does well on a test, she'll say, "This will matter for years, I am the one who made this happen, and this will affect many aspects of my life." A pessimist will say, "I won't do well on the next test, it was easy so everyone did well, and it is only one little subject." The opposite is true of failure or a negative experience - for the optimist the negative experience is short term, occurred through lack of effort, and is isolated. Simply recognizing that there are multiple views for any experience or situation is an important step in building optimism.

GIVE YOURSELF:

CREATE EMPATHY

Empathy is the ability to recognize and respond to other people's emotions. It is connected to optimism because it is through a sense of our connection to others that we see our own efficacy and importance. Together they govern a significant portion of our behavior; they are the gatekeepers of our emotional selves. When we are empathic, it hurts us to hurt others or to see them hurt. We actually experience for ourselves the emotions of others. It is motivating, then, not only to do what makes us feel good, but what makes others feel good. Thus, empathy is the force which makes the golden rule true. Some parts of empathy are instinctive. Infants will reach out and touch others in distress; in maternity wards, one infant's tears will lead to a room full of crying babies. This mimicry is the first step towards forming empathy. Unfortunately, this unconscious or instinctive behavior does not automatically lead to conscious empathy. Instead, these flickering flames must be carefully banked and fueled through role-modeling, reinforcement, and practice. Once people develop empathy on a conscious level, it becomes self-reinforcing because it answers a deep-seated need to build sustaining relationships with others.

COMMIT TO NOBLE GOALS

Noble goals activate all of the other elements of EQ. Through our missions, our callings, and our acts of human kindness, the commitment to emotional intelligence gains relevance and power. Just as our personal priorities shape our daily choices, our noble goals shape our long-term choices. They give us a sense of direction, they give us a spar to hold in the storm, and they are the compass for our soul.

Recently, we were flying to a conference and sat with a remarkable man who manages a factory that produces circuit breakers. He told us about the rewards and strategies he uses to manage and motivate his teams; this man is clearly a gifted manager with great insight and well-developed skills. We talked about how motivated his employees might become if they knew how their efforts were making the world better. Are their breakers used in Red Cross hospitals keeping children alive? Then the team should know.

The manager explained that their product is one of the most dependable on the market, so it is used in many agricultural applications. His team is helping to feed our entire nation. His team helps keep farmers in business. His team helps nourish the very roots of our nation. Realizing this importance, he decided he'd go back to the plant and make sure every member of his team knew the importance of their work.

All the "inside" aspects of emotional intelligence change your attitudes, they shape your own life; they help you become the person you want to be. Your noble goals touch the future.

PUTTING IT TOGETHER

Now that you have some idea of what we mean by emotional intelligence and what this book is about, it is time to start practicing. It only takes a bit of time each day, perhaps six seconds at a time, to start making a significant difference in your life and the lives of the people around you. Celebrate the possibilities and enjoy exploring this book.

Emotional
Intelligence

Courage

Adversity

Perseverance

Interdependence

Empathy

Creativity

Noble Goal

Motivation

Curiosity

Accountability

Optimism

Forgiveness

Initiative

Conflict

Humor

Tolerance

Service

Truth

Tranquility

Awareness

Resiliency

Self-Control

Fusion

Integrity

It takes courage to get up every morning, to face your day, to live life. It takes courage to make a friend or talk to the neighbor. It takes courage to start kindergarten, it takes courage to start a new job, it takes courage to follow your vision, and it takes courage to change yourself.

You have to be a risk taker to participate in life in any way or you will live your life in isolation. At the same time, fear can be healthy — there are many dangers to respect. Just do not live a life defined by fears.

Courage comes from hope and optimism. It can come from faith, it can come from a sense of purpose. It also takes many forms, large and small. The important thing is not so much being a hero as it is doing what is right. We practice on the small things, and eventually we can look back and see the big picture.

Courage

Courage Activities

- There are Courage Feather stickers in the back of this book. Place the large one someplace you will see it every day to remember this theme. Use the small ones on days you need an extra "boost" of courage.

- Institute a family "show and tell" time where children can try out the monthly value at school and then be a "star" at home when they share that success.

- Create a family/home "art gallery" where you will celebrate emotional intelligence themes or values by creating a work of art.

- Pick a small challenge like talking to a grouchy neighbor or going someplace new. Keep a record of the new challenges you face and see if they become more and more significant and/or easier to face.

- Consider an activity or risk you did not take recently. List the reasons why. Are these excuses made out of fear or are they real reasons? See how many excuses you can eliminate with courage.

- Get involved with someone new. Invite someone you don't know well for lunch. Sit next to someone in the cafeteria or lunch room whom you don't know.

- Follow your conscience and be an advocate for someone who is being criticized or not listened too — even if they are not popular.

- Sometimes when people are afraid, they say, "I do not want to do this." Instead, try to say, "I do want to do this — but I am afraid." This separation allows the motivation to exist alongside the fear.

- It is overwhelming to face some fears "head on." For instance, if a child is afraid to sleep over at a friend's house, maybe the two friends can have an overnight in the first child's living room. Gradual steps!

- Keep a special plate in the cupboard, and use it to celebrate acts of courage. Whoever conquers a fear gets to use the special plate at dinner.

> "Courage is the first of human qualities because it is
> the quality which guarantees all the others."
> — Winston Churchill

Emotional Intelligence

Courage

Adversity

Perseverance

Interdependence

Empathy

Creativity

Noble Goal

Motivation

Curiosity

Accountability

Optimism

Forgiveness

Initiative

Conflict

Humor

Tolerance

Service

Truth

Tranquility

Awareness

Resiliency

Self-Control

Fusion

Integrity

Courage Quotes

"One doesn't discover new lands without consenting to lose sight of the shore for a very long time."
— André Gide

"In Chinese, the word crisis is wei ji, composed of the character wei, which means danger, and ji, which means opportunity."
— Jan Wong

"Life shrinks or expands in proportion to one's courage."
— Anaïs Nin

"Behold the turtle. He only makes progress when he sticks his neck out."
— James Bryant Conant

Research says...

Silence can be a barometer for timidity. Reserved, silent children can be at risk for developing anxiety disorders. Act as a mentor or coach to encourage gradually emboldening experiences.

Courage Fusion Questions

Who was more courageous — Ferdinand Magellan or Alan Shepherd? How about Mother Teresa or Winston Churchill?

Which is more courageous — rainbows or daffodils?

Which part of the courage collage (on page 12) shows real courage?

What does courage promote? What are its effects?

Why are you courageous some days but not others?

Which takes more courage — to tell the truth to others or to admit the truth to yourself?

Courage Inspiration

Role Models

Charles Litke was a Chaplain in Vietnam and winner of the Congressional Medal of Honor who left his medal at The Wall in protest of US military action in Central America. Now he travels to observe and call attention to the effects of US foreign policy in Latin America.

Sir Thomas Moore was killed because he would not change his beliefs to suit the King. He has become a symbol of the conflict between two loyalties — he loved his King, but he would not renounce his faith.

Yitzhak Rabin initiated peace negotiations with the PLO and was killed by a radical opposed to compromise. Rabin's courage required him to face his allies as well as his former enemies.

Books and Movies For Younger People

The Journey of Natty Gann, Disney — a young girl travels across the Depression-bound country in search of her father.

Hatchet, Gary Paulsen — a boy survives alone after a plane crash in the Canadian Rockies.

The Rescuers, Disney — The Rescue Aid Society comes to save a young girl — but in the end it takes her courage to save the day.

The Wild Children, Felice Holman — homeless children struggle to survive after the Russian Revolution.

Books and Movies For Older People

Into Thin Air, John Krakauer — facing death and redemption on Mt. Everest.

Schindler's List, Stephen Spielberg — a German man stands alone to rescue persecuted Jews.

West With The Night, Beryl Markham — living in Africa, facing life, and taking risks.

Julia — Jane Fonda and Vanessa Redgrave star in this drama about a foreign writer who helps the resistance in Nazi Germany.

Emotional
Intelligence

Courage

Adversity

Perseverance

Interdependence

Empathy

Creativity

Noble Goal

Motivation

Curiosity

Accountability

Optimism

Forgiveness

Initiative

Conflict

Humor

Tolerance

Service

Truth

Tranquility

Awareness

Resiliency

Self-Control

Fusion

Integrity

"Although the world is full of suffering it is also full of the overcoming of it."
—Helen Keller

Adversity

Research shows that of the people who go on to make significant change in their chosen field, the majority faced great adversity growing up.

We do not choose many of the events and circumstances of our lives, but we do control how we react to them. Adversity is always difficult, but for some it is also an opportunity. Adversity is like a forge where our true beliefs are challenged, then strengthened. As Buddha said, life is full of pain — and we can choose to suffer or to grow.

When you are in pain, know that you are not alone, and that when you overcome the crisis you will be stronger. Then, share that strength with another.

Adversity Activities

• Write for 15 minutes for five days about a traumatic experience or ongoing challenge. Research shows that the net effect is enhanced immune function, so that should be incentive to keep on going!

• Faced with adversity, we often look to place blame. When children are sad, for example, they often talk about what someone else did. To grow from adversity we must identify the changes we will make in ourselves rather than the changes we want others to make. Make a chart with two columns, one for yourself and one for others. Write what changes you would like to see, and move as many as possible to the "me" column.

• List all the bad things that are happening. Now list a good thing for each bad thing. You can make this a journal entry, or write three good things that happen on every day of your calendar this month.

• Make a special box to keep all the positive messages, thank you notes, and friendly messages you receive. Go through them when you feel down.

• Exercise has been proven to help manage stress. If you do not feel up to "exercise," try just getting outside and going for walks.

• Do community service. Helping people makes us feel connected, effective, and gives meaning to our lives. Look in the phone book or newspaper for ideas on where to volunteer (see "Service" in this book).

• Drawing, painting, sculpting, or other creative pursuits can have a powerful therapeutic effect. You can directly express emotions and frustrations then expunge them by tearing up the work. You can envision a positive future, or you can dwell in the moment of creation. This work is not necessarily for anyone else to see, and is appropriate for people of all ages. If you find that you resist "doing art," try simply creating images of your thoughts and feelings.

• Find a place in nature. Sit under a tree, look at a plant, watch the water flow, or even build an imaginary natural haven. This connection builds a place of safety and a tie to generations of past and future people who are also a part of nature.

• Go to a plant nursery and ask if they will donate a sickly plant to you for nursing. Recognize that you may not be able to save it, but provide it with the most personal, solicitous care possible, and monitor your results. Return to the nursery for further help and/or to celebrate your success.

Emotional
Intelligence

Courage

Adversity

Perseverance

Interdependence

Empathy

Creativity

Noble Goal

Motivation

Curiosity

Accountability

Optimism

Forgiveness

Initiative

Conflict

Humor

Tolerance

Service

Truth

Tranquility

Awareness

Resiliency

Self-Control

Fusion

Integrity

Adversity Quotes

"We who lived in concentration camps can remember the men who walked through the huts comforting others, giving away their last piece of bread. They may have been few in number, but they offer sufficient proof that everything can be taken from a man but one thing: the last of human freedoms — to choose one's attitude in any given circumstances — to choose one's own way." — Viktor Frankl

"The burden is equal to the horse's strength." — The Talmud

"Sorrow is a fruit; God does not allow it to grow on a branch that is too weak to bear it." — Victor Hugo

"You are a child of the universe no less than the trees and the stars; you have a right to be here." — Max Ehrmann

"Emotion, which is suffering, ceases to be suffering as soon as we have a clear picture of it." — Spinoza

Research says...

To reduce depression, we have to learn to dispute with ourselves. Arguing multiple sides of an issue helps build the awareness that most crises are **temporary**, **isolated**, and can be changed through additional **effort** (TIE).

Females suffer from depression twice as often as men. The three principle explanations are: 1) learned helplessness; 2) too much rumination; and 3) the pursuit of thinness (95% of women fail in attempts to diet).

Adversity Questions

Why did many American prisoners of war during Vietnam return with a higher IQ than before their imprisonment?

In the movie *Ordinary People,* the psychiatrist says, "If you can't feel pain, you can't feel anything at all." What does that mean? How true is this opinion?

Buddha said the first noble truth is "suffering" or "life is pain." Does that mean we can never have happiness? Why?

Which suffers more adversity — the river or the rock? Which gains more from the adversity?

Adversity Inspiration

Role Models

Nelson Mandela kept his vision of a united, non-segregated South Africa alive despite 27 years of imprisonment. Through the efforts of dedicated citizens, he was able to direct the efforts of the ANC to create an equal rights revolution in his country. Amandala.

Viktor Frankl survived the Holocaust and went on to write the lessons of the experience.

Aung San Suukyi won the 1991 Nobel Peace Prize for her work protesting for human rights in Myanmar despite years of persecution and jail. She used the Nobel funds to create a trust for health and education.

The picture above is Josh's sister, Debbie, teaching in rural Kenya. Like millions of volunteers each year, she and her husband chose to serve in difficult conditions because they were needed.

Books and Movies For Younger People

 I Can Hear the Sun, Patricia Polacco — a homeless boy discovers love and acceptance by helping the geese in the park.

 The Acorn People, Ron Jones — a young man learns to see beyond the disabilities of children in summer camp.

 Eggbert the Slightly Cracked Egg, Ross and Barron — despite a crack and the discrimination he faces, Eggbert finds a place in the world and shares his talents.

 Lorenzo's Oil (PG13) — when the Odones learn their son has a rare terminal disease, they must find new reserves of strength and commitment.

Books and Movies For Older People

 Yellow Raft in Blue Water, Michael Dorris —when there are no other options, a young woman, her mother, and grandmother all find their strengths.

 City of Joy — in the most desperate conditions in Calcutta, people remain humane and supportive and create a remarkable community.

Emotional Intelligence

Courage

Adversity

Perseverance

Interdependence

Empathy

Creativity

Noble Goal

Motivation

Curiosity

Accountability

Optimism

Forgiveness

Initiative

Conflict

Humor

Tolerance

Service

Truth

Tranquility

Awareness

Resiliency

Self-Control

Fusion

Integrity

Perseverance

Perseverance is the only emotional attribute that directly correlates with IQ. In other words, if you have more perseverance, you will have a higher IQ. Actually, it isn't surprising because thinking is hard work.

Perseverance is also an emotional attribute that affects every aspect of our daily lives. Ready to give up? We hope not, because when you have that feeling it is most likely time for you to do just the opposite. Luckily, you can increase your perseverance. Unfortunately, this is not an easy task — it takes an ongoing commitment.

One aspect of this growth is accepting that it is reasonable and worthwhile to engage in the hard work of perseverance. One key step is transferring satisfaction from "I'll do this because it is enjoyable," to "I'll do this because meeting my responsibilities is satisfying." Thus, it is important for people, including children, to experience relevant **meaningful** responsibilities with built-in consequences.

Perseverance

Perseverance Activities

• Create a perseverance contract with someone. You choose a task or activity in which you need to persevere, s/he does the same. Your contract should include deadlines, a date to check progress, and celebrations along the way.

• When you are frustrated and ready to give up, think of ten other ways of solving this particular problem. Think back on five times when you solved a problem and consider your track record. Imagine how you would move forward if you had all the help you needed. Think what it will feel like to have solved this problem. Often, simply seeing the end of the tunnel is enough to get you through.

• Break a task down into "baby steps." It takes practice to make challenges "bite size," so try it before you're at the end of your rope.

• When you have made a mistake, identify the reasons why it is temporary and specific to the situation. In other words, be clear that you may have a failure, but you are not a failure. Failure is an event, not a person.

• Accept a physical challenge like orienteering, rock climbing, or mountain biking.

• Often families will create a plan to solve a problem, but when it appears ineffective, they give it up. Remember that no system will work immediately or 100% of the time, so persevere.

• Mail yourself a postcard congratulating yourself on how you persevered and accomplished a difficult change, **then** focus on making this goal happen. Depending on the challenge, you might hide the card away for a month or a year.

• In the back of the book is a set of 21 stickers to help build a new habit. Research shows that if you consistently apply a new habit for 21 days, it will become much easier to continue the behavior.

• Model the importance of backtracking or starting over. When an accident (e.g., spilled milk) occurs, clean up, then go back to the beginning.

• Adopt a pet (e.g., goldfish, or hampster) and have your child participate **with** you in the daily care. Over time, shift the responsibility for initiation to the child, but maintain the shared job.

Emotional
Intelligence
Courage
Adversity
Perseverance
Interdependence
Empathy
Creativity
Noble Goal
Motivation
Curiosity
Accountability
Optimism
Forgiveness
Initiative
Conflict
Humor
Tolerance
Service
Truth
Tranquility
Awareness
Resiliency
Self-Control
Fusion
Integrity

Michael Leahy, 46, was diagnosed with terminal melanoma just before he was to compete in the Ironman marathon in Hawai'i. His doctors said he had from six weeks to six months to live. He competed anyway, finishing the race in just over 13 hours. Immediately after crossing the finish line, he promised to compete in the next Ironman as an affirmation of his will to live.

Perseverance Quotes

"He who would learn to fly one day must first learn to stand and walk and run and climb and dance; one cannot fly into flying."

— Fredrich Nietzsche

"If you won't be better tomorrow than you were today, then what do you need tomorrow for?"

— Rabbi Nahman of Btatslav

Research says...

According to a Carnegie Council report, many parents disengage from their teenagers too soon. As a result, kids are left to drift and sometimes get into trouble with nobody nearby to notice. Even when teens loudly proclaim their need for independence and actively reject you, they still need you to hang in there with them.

Perseverance Fusion Questions

Why is the word "severe" in "perseverance"?

Which took more perseverance — the nautilus seashell or the black sand beach in the photo to the right?

What is the difference between perseverance and motivation?

Can someone else "give" you perseverance?

Why isn't it easy to persevere?

Is perseverance always positive?

What would motivate you to increase your perseverance?

Perseverance Inspiration

Role Models

Albert Einstein is known as a remarkable genius but he was also learning disabled. He compensated for his learning style through remarkable perseverance.

The liquid cleanser "409" is so named because the first 408 attempts failed.

Books and Movies For Younger People

 Iron Will — a young man competes in a grueling dog sled race where he must prove his will.

 The Incredible Journey — three pets support each other and find their way home despite overwhelming odds.

 Bunny Cakes, Rosemary Wells — Max struggles, tries and tries again until he finally can buy red hot marshmallow squirters.

Books and Movies For Older People

 Autobiography of a Face, Lucy Grealy — a woman's struggle to shed society's concern with image; she learned to look through the mirrors to see herself.

 Moving Violations, John Hockenberry — a journalist refuses to be defined by his disabilities (he is paraplegic); he takes any assignment and travels the world as an ace reporter.

Emotional Intelligence
Courage
Adversity
Perseverance
Interdependence
Empathy
Creativity
Noble Goal
Motivation
Curiosity
Accountability
Optimism
Forgiveness
Initiative
Conflict
Humor
Tolerance
Service
Truth
Tranquility
Awareness
Resiliency
Self-Control
Fusion
Integrity

INTERDE

"When the oak is felled
the forest echoes
with its fall,

All life is twined in an intricate
web. When one strand is
changed, the whole changes. As
we learn to see beyond ourselves, we recognize the
connections that we have to other people and the effects we have on one
another.

Interdependence is a strength. It is a partnership, it is community. To
be effective, though, all individuals must recognize their commitments
and must be ready to act with integrity. Covey writes that interdependence is a choice only independent people can make. This balance
requires honesty, humility, and patience.

Interdependence

Interdependence Activities

Emotional
Intelligence

Courage

Adversity

Perseverance

Interdependence

Empathy

Creativity

Noble Goal

Motivation

Curiosity

Accountability

Optimism

Forgiveness

Initiative

Conflict

Humor

Tolerance

Service

Truth

Tranquility

Awareness

Resiliency

Self-Control

Fusion

Integrity

• Consider your relationships with other people, or with nature, and evaluate each on a scale from 1 to 10 in terms of the quality of interdependence. Pick one with a low score and identify one step you will take to improve the relationship.

t a hundred acorns

sown silently

an unnoticed breeze."

— Thomas Carlyle

• Discuss family dilemmas or current event problems and brainstorm "win-win" solutions. Write up current events solutions and send them to the editor of your paper.

• Go one week — or maybe just a day — with no help from anyone on anything.

• Getting a "yes" in negotiation requires that we put ourselves in the other person's shoes. Pick someone you disagree with and identify ten feelings he may have that create his point of view.

• Use a roll of yarn to create a web of relationships in your home or community. Label the threads and explore how each point of the web depends on and helps the others.

• One day, or one vacation, carry a stack of.postcards and write as many "thank you cards" as you can possibly manage. Write a note to everyone who is kind, helpful, or positive.

• Create a "block party" activity in your neighborhood; it could be a progressive picnic organized by kids, an Olympics, or maybe a summer-time waterplay festival.

• Write a postcard to someone with whom you totally disagree. Ask for her/his ideas on a complex problem you are working with, and see if there is stimulating, surprising, or valuable insight.

Interdependence Quotes

"We have committed the Golden Rule to memory; let us now commit it to life."

— Edwin Markham

"Man does not weave this web of life. He is merely a strand of it. Whatever he does to the web, he does to himself."

— Chief Seattle

"People treat us the way we teach them to treat us." — Wayne Dyer

Research says...

Healthy interdependence is tied to the attachment and bonding process. According to Fahlberg, a child who is well bonded to her/his primary caregiver will have a stronger sense of conscience and more positive relationships. Bonding develops when a child's needs are met by her/his caregiver and when love is demonstrated through touch, facial expression, and/or eye contact.

Interdependence Fusion Questions

Do you gain freedom or loose freedom by accepting interdependence?

In the picture below, you can see a buffalo (it is "Yellowstone Christmas, August 25, 1989). How does this photo show interdependence?

Can you create interdependence with someone who wants to be independent from you?

If you were making an illustration for interdependence, what image(s) would you use? What would you want to make people feel?

Which is more interdependent — a circle or a square?

Interdependence Inspiration

Role Models

Sojourner Truth was an active abolitionist and feminist in the 1800's.

Jimmy Carter rallies support for low income housing and still actively works to create a more equitable society.

Brigham Young organized thousands of pioneers to trek across the plains with a "pyramid plan" that ensured care and support for all.

Desmond Tutu won the 1984 Nobel Peace Prize for his work against apartheid in South Africa.

Books and Movies For Younger People

 Hoosiers — a movie that celebrates the power of teamwork.

 Unstrung Heroes — a 12 year old connects with his unusual uncles as he comes to terms with a dying mother and distant father.

 Dragonsong Trilogy, Anne McCaffrey — a girl overcomes sexism to become a force for good.

 Walk Two Moons, Sharon Creech — on a road trip with her grandparents, a girl learns about family.

Books and Movies For Older People

 The Lions of Al Rassan, Guy Gavriel Kay — in a world torn by war, a young doctor weaves the story of the two warriors she loves.

 The Forest People, Colin Turnbull — the story of a society that is truly interdependent.

The Englishman Who Went Up a Hill & Came Down a Mountain — a town works together to build a mountain and put themselves "on the map."

Emotional Intelligence

Courage

Adversity

Perseverance

Interdependence

Empathy

Creativity

Noble Goal

Motivation

Curiosity

Accountability

Optimism

Forgiveness

Initiative

Conflict

Humor

Tolerance

Service

Truth

Tranquility

Awareness

Resiliency

Self-Control

Fusion

Integrity

> "In a full heart
> there is room for
> everything, and
> in an empty one,
> there is room for
> nothing."
>
> — Antonio Porchia

Empathy allows us to reach beyond our own individual experiences by feeling what other people experience. Goleman writes, "Empathy leads to caring, altruism, and compassion. Seeing things from another's perspective breaks down biased stereotypes, and so breeds tolerance and acceptance of difference."

Empathy is also critical to communication. When we communicate, much of the "message" is in the tone of voice and body language. In fact, when we communicate emotions, 90% or more of the "message" is nonverbal. So, we need to become more fluent in this kind of communication.

Empathy Activities

- With younger children, make up a "charades" guessing game. One person guesses the emotion the other person is demonstrating.

- Experiment with nonverbal communication by saying the same words in different ways. Try to identify how tone and body language change the communication.

- Sometimes it is easier to empathize with characters or animals who won't disagree with you. When you are reading or watching TV discuss what the characters are feeling and why. How would you resolve their problems?

- Role play by acting out a conflict, then try switching roles.

- Volunteer to work at the Special Olympics, or just attend. Website: www.specialolympics.org

- Make sure your children have the opportunity to interact with all kinds of people. Go to different parks and playgrounds, and visit several schools.

- When a child receives a gift, have her or him choose another possession to give away. Or, suggest a child choose one of their most prized possessions as a gift for someone who needs it even more.

- Try eating a meal blindfolded or with a hand tied behind your back.

- Take a homeless person out for a meal.

- Set aside an hour to <u>really</u> <u>listen</u> to someone.

- Do you completely, totally, absolutely disagree with someone? Next time you have a disagreement, send a postcard saying, "Even though we disagree, I understand and respect (or acknowledge) the way you feel."

- Make a set of feeling "flashcards" with people and faces showing different emotions. Discuss what blend of emotions is apparent in each.

- Experiment with making yourself feel different emotions by remembering events, places, and people. Watch yourself in a mirror or on video and see if you can observe changes in your own face and body as your emotions change.

Emotional Intelligence
Courage
Adversity
Perseverance
Interdependence
Empathy
Creativity
Noble Goal
Motivation
Curiosity
Accountability
Optimism
Forgiveness
Initiative
Conflict
Humor
Tolerance
Service
Truth
Tranquility
Awareness
Resiliency
Self-Control
Fusion
Integrity

Empathy Quotes

"The important thing is being capable of emotions, but to experience only one's own would be a sorry limitation."   — Andre Gide

"All learning has an emotional base."   — Plato

"Nobody has ever measured, not even poets, how much the heart can hold."
          — Zelda Fitzgerald

"What comes from the heart, goes to the heart."
          — Samuel Taylor Coleridge

"I follow my heart for I can trust it."   — J. C. F. von Schiller

Research Says...

It takes only 1/24th of a second to correctly interpret facial expressions.

Research shows that increasing the ability to read nonverbal messages correlates directly with higher popularity, grades, and even a better love life.

Empathy Fusion Questions

Do you act more empathic toward those you love or toward strangers?

If people could be so empathic that they knew exactly what other people felt, would crime still exist?

What's the difference between empathy and forgiveness?

Are females "naturally" more empathic than males? Does one gender usually act more empathic?

Which is more important to you — to have people to understand how you feel, or for you to understand how other people feel?

Can someone ever actually understand how someone else is feeling?

What is the difference between sympathy and empathy?

Empathy Inspiration

Role Models

Amnesty International was created to call attention to the suffering of individuals at the hands of governments.

Clara Barton founded the Red Cross to relieve suffering from the ravages of war.

Robin Williams, Whoopi Goldberg, Billy Crystal, and other artists have created programs such as *Comic Relief* to help victims of poverty and homelessness.

Books and Movies For Younger People

 Ender's Game, Orson Scott Card — a boy is raised to destroy an alien race, and comes to understand rather than hate them.

The Bear — a touching tale of a cub who learns to live on his own..

The Giver, Lowis Lowery — in a society where no one feels pain, one child inherits the suffering of all.

Books and Movies For Older People

Paula, Isabel Allende — a woman gives her family history as a farewell gift to her daughter.

Emerald Eyes, Daniel Keys Moran — the "gift" of telepathy is cruel in this future.

Children of a Lesser God, Mark Medoff — a teacher learns that his deaf students can not be defined by their disabilities.

Emotional
Intelligence

Courage

Adversity

Perseverance

Interdependence

Empathy

Creativity

Noble Goal

Motivation

Curiosity

Accountability

Optimism

Forgiveness

Initiative

Conflict

Humor

Tolerance

Service

Truth

Tranquility

Awareness

Resiliency

Self-Control

Fusion

Integrity

Creativity is piercing the mundane to find the marv

— Bill Moyers

Creativity

When we have conflict or no one seems to be hearing what we're saying, it is time for some creativity.

Fear activates the limbic system at the base of our brains. This shuts off the cerebral cortex, where creativity lives. Love is the antidote to fear and the wellspring of creativity.

Creativity is not so much making something new as it is recombining the old. Creativity requires informality because its essence is "breaking rules." The result is that creativity is sometimes tied to strong emotions which both give it power and make it challenging.

As we strive to make sense of our world, there is a great deal that fits in neither words nor logic. Creativity allows us to tap the seed of human experience and express that ineffable blossom.

Creativity Activities

- Have a backwards day, beginning by having dinner for breakfast.

- Use a copier or computer to enlarge small objects and shrink big ones. Make a collage.

- Explore how two or more ideas can be put together. Create an ongoing practice after dinner or in the car where you use this kind of thinking (it is called biosciation).

- Ask your child, or anyone else, open-ended questions rather than closed ones. An open-ended question does not have a single or "right" answer; for instance, "What was interesting in your day?" instead of "Did you have a good day?"

- Make a sculpture, fort, or costume by using everyday items in unusual ways. Turn a couch on its side or bring garden furniture inside.

- Make up a card game. You can start by changing a game you know, then change it again.

- Play mental games like "what if...." These require a willingness to think freely, so you need to practice not closing the door on ideas. Resist ever saying, "Don't be silly!" or "That's a stupid question." If a question seems silly, maybe it is time for a silly answer, but don't close the door.

- Try cooking with new and unusual spices which you've never used. Use the smells to guide your culinary exploration.

- Get on the internet and play a game where you follow links not based on what information is presented, but on the first letter of the link. See what random and amusing sites you find.

- Create a model of an environment in which you'd like to live. Use only found objects and natural materials.

- Make your own "magnetic poetry" using favorite words. You can buy a self-adhesive magnetic sheet from many sign-making shops.

- Have a tea party or an event where each guest plays the part of a character from a book, movie, the media, or other realm.

Emotional
Intelligence
Courage
Adversity
Perseverance
Interdependence
Empathy
Creativity
Noble Goal
Motivation
Curiosity
Accountability
Optimism
Forgiveness
Initiative
Conflict
Humor
Tolerance
Service
Truth
Tranquility
Awareness
Resiliency
Self-Control
Fusion
Integrity

Creativity Quotes

"If you ask me what I came to do in this world, I, an artist, I will answer you: 'I am here to live out loud.'"

— Emille Zola

"Art is the invisible made visible."

— Peter Brook

"The universe is made up of stories not atoms."
— Muriel Rukeyser

"Art washes away from the soul the dust of everyday life." — Pablo Picasso

Research Says...

Humor unleashes creativity. In a study, a group who watched TV bloopers became more inventive than a group who was taught techniques of creativity.

Creativity Fusion Questions

Which is more creative — a sunflower or an ostrich? A milkshake or a float? A beautiful painting or a beautiful relationship? Why?

Which would be more creative — the most wonderful, smooth, clean and effective car imaginable, or a sculpture that captured the essence of love in a totally unique way?

Does anyone create **new** ideas, or just rediscover old ones?

How separate are your left and right brains? Is there a "logical" kind of creativity?

Which is harder — starting a creative project, or finishing it? Why?

Is the kind of creativity that lets people solve problems fundamentally different than the creativity to make art?

Creativity Inspiration

Role Models

Many artists are remarkably creative. Spend some time in a museum and see who inspires you.

Buckminster Fuller, architect, creator of geodesic dome.

Torville and Dean brought pairs ice-skating to a new level of choreographic ingenuity.

Elizabeth Cady Stanton organized the first women's rights convention.

Books and Movies For Younger People

 Fantasia, Disney — a landscape of imagination and art.

 Little Man Tate — a genius boy who is encouraged to explore.

Appelemando's Dreams, Patricia Polacco — a boy's dreams fill the air with color and teach the town to see.

The Fantastic Drawings of Danielle, Barbara McClintock — a young artist sees the fantastic, and those she loves learn to accept her unique vision.

Books and Movies For Older People

 Apollo 13 — an adventure of expanding horizons with an incredible moment of creativity when the air filters must be repaired without parts.

 Shine — the conflict between an artist's need to create and the pressure for perfection.

Zen and the Art of Motorcycle Maintenance, Robert Pirsig — new ways of looking and thinking.

"The trouble with specialists is that they tend to think in grooves."
— Elaine Morgan

Emotional
Intelligence

Courage

Adversity

Perseverance

Interdependence

Empathy

Creativity

Noble Goal

Motivation

Curiosity

Accountability

Optimism

Forgiveness

Initiative

Conflict

Humor

Tolerance

Service

Truth

Tranquility

Awareness

Resiliency

Self-Control

Fusion

Integrity

Noble Goal

Know thyself — Socrate
Choose thyself — Kierkega
Give thyself — Jesus

A **noble goal** is a goal with a healthy dose of idealism. It reaches beyond you, beyond individuals, beyond family, and helps you measure all of your decisions. Sometimes a noble goal is called a mission, a higher purpose, or a set of ideals.

Sometimes it is difficult to see if a goal is noble. Some goals seem valuable, but it is easy to get caught up in an effort that might be selfish. A noble goal doesn't profit one individual over another and doesn't hurt anyone — it improves the quality of life for all.

Noble Goal Activities

• Make a list of your personal beliefs or philosophy. What principles should govern every day of your life? Put the list away for awhile, then come back to it and decide how you would feel about a person who lived this way.

• Make a list of what the world needs. Pick one idea a week and see if you can use that **need** as a noble goal. When you find a need that helps you decide what is right in your daily life, make a sign and hang it somewhere to remind you of your noble goal.

• Read some mission statements from businesses, churches, schools, and organizations. Write a mission statement for yourself or with your family.

• Participate in an activity that serves a noble goal, such as Earth Day, Wee Care, or literacy tutoring. Imagine if ten million people joined you — wouldn't you like to live in that world?

• Make it a habit to always be creating a hat, scarf, or blanket to give away to someone in need.

• Time yourself for one minute and write down a list in answer to this question: If I had unlimited time and resources, what would I do? (Dream. Write down every idea that surfaces.)

• Create a special time, perhaps on a holiday, where each year your family (or you) reflects on your noble goals, revises them, and recommits.

• Send a postcard to a person or organization whose goal you admire.

• Have a family/team/group discussion about the positive and negative aspects of both selfishness and altruism. What if everybody in the world were more selfish? Or selfish but with a long-term view? Is "goodness" tied to giving? After the discussion, have each person set a non-materialistic goal.

• Analyze your relationships. Do you have any "I win/you lose" relationships? What are you teaching that individual? Can you shift more relationships to "win-win"?

• Pick an individual to respectfully observe. What can you learn about this person's values and goals simply from observing?

Emotional
Intelligence
Courage
Adversity
Perseverance
Interdependence
Empathy
Creativity
Noble Goal
Motivation
Curiosity
Accountability
Optimism
Forgiveness
Initiative
Conflict
Humor
Tolerance
Service
Truth
Tranquility
Awareness
Resiliency
Self-Control
Fusion
Integrity

Noble Goal Quotes

"One thing I know: the only ones among you who will be really happy are those who will have sought and found how to serve."
—Albert Schweitzer

"You have not converted a man because you have silenced him."
— John Manley

"The greatest despair is to not become the person you were meant to be."
— Kierkegaard

Research Says...

The competitive nature of American culture encourages ranking. It is easy to believe that we are better than others. We tend to judge **ourselves** based on our intentions (even when our actions do not follow suit), while we judge **others** on their actions (and ignore their intentions).

Noble Goal Fusion Questions

If you were able to convince every person you knew to work for a whole year doing something good, what would you ask them to do?

If you could place a sign in every classroom in your country, knowing the students would read it every day, what would your sign say?

Which is harder — to do great acts of kindness each month, or small acts every hour? Which makes more difference?

Can a goal still be a "noble goal" if some people don't like it — or don't like you for pursuing it?

What keeps your noble goal from being real tomorrow?

Who is remembered by history — people who pursued noble goals or people who pursued selfish goals? Why is that? Whose history is it?

Noble Goal Inspiration

Role Models

Candy Litener created MADD to meet her noble goal of stopping death from drunk driving.

Martin Luther King, Jr. had the noble goal so eloquently expressed as his dream — a color-blind America.

Florence Nightingale's noble goal was humane, careful, and compassionate medical care.

Mother Teresa's noble goal was serving the poorest of the poor in their greatest hours of need.

Books and Movies For Younger People

 Peace Crane, Sheila Hamanaka — 50 years after Hiroshima, an affirmation of the spirit of Sadako and the promise of peace.

 The Miracle Worker, William Gibson — an inspiring play and a movie about Annie Sullivan teaching blind Helen Keller.

 Star Wars — the struggle of good against an overwhelming force of evil.

Books and Movies For Older People

 In the Time of the Butterflies, Julia Alvarez — four sisters sacrifice comfort in the name of freedom.

 The Milagro Beanfield War — a community must decide whether wealth or tradition is more important.

 Citizen Kane — an Orson Welles film about Hearst's responsibility as a journalist.

 Dead Poet's Society — Robin Williams is a teacher whose energy and passion for truth awakens his students.

Emotional
Intelligence

Courage

Adversity

Perseverance

Interdependence

Empathy

Creativity

Noble Goal

Motivation

Curiosity

Accountability

Optimism

Forgiveness

Initiative

Conflict

Humor

Tolerance

Service

Truth

Tranquility

Awareness

Resiliency

Self-Control

Fusion

Integrity

Change your habits, change the world.

Motivation

There are many kinds of motivation. Extrinsic motivations come from hope of recognition or reward. Intrinsic motivations come from a sense of purpose. They are, ultimately, inseparable, so it makes sense to use them together.

One of the biggest motivators is the sense that we have control. So, if you want to increase the motivation of students, family, or colleagues, give them choices in their duties and responsibilities. Choice can be as simple as the order of tasks or the method of presenting work. Another key motivator is knowing that our actions will make a difference.

Twenty years of research on motivation and achievement bears out the idea of "self-fulfilling prophecy." Aim for the stars because we tend to be, do, and accomplish what we think we can.

Motivation Activities

- Pick something you have always wanted to do — learning a skill, playing an instrument, creating a project — schedule the time, and do it!

- When a child or friend comes to you with a problem, don't fix it. (This is hard! Be strict with yourself.) Instead, support her and help her understand the problem. Offer her encouragement to generate her own solution(s).

- Make sure your child has real choice about important matters in the family. Make sure there are areas of children's lives in which they have total control. Also, ensure that child-input is a part of the family decision-making process.

- Spontaneous and unexpected rewards build internal motivation. When someone you love does something well, have a special celebration, buy a popsicle, put up streamers, throw confetti.

- Negotiated incentives and consequences are effective when they are consistent and when both (or all) parties agree. Create a reward system for yourself, your family, or your workplace. There can be many stages of reward from: "If we are on time all day we'll have ice cream," to, "If we get this project done on time, everybody gets three days off." The overlapping combination of short term and long term, big and small, is most effective.

- Pick three activities you love to do and list the reasons you are motivated to perform those activities; can you use those motivations someplace else?

- List all of your actions and activities from the last 24 hours, and sort them into "what I chose" and "what others chose for me."

"If you won't be better tomorrow than you were today, then what do you need tomorrow for?"

— Rabbi Nahman of Braslav

Emotional Intelligence
Courage
Adversity
Perseverance
Interdependence
Empathy
Creativity
Noble Goal
Motivation
Curiosity
Accountability
Optimism
Forgiveness
Initiative
Conflict
Humor
Tolerance
Service
Truth
Tranquility
Awareness
Resiliency
Self-Control
Fusion
Integrity

Motivation Quotes

"The key to motivation is having a motive — having a <u>why</u>."
— Stephen Covey

"All people by nature desire to learn."
—Aristotle

"Words show a man's wit, but actions show his meaning."
— Werner Erhard

"Science may have found a cure for many evils; but it has found no remedy for the worst of them all — the apathy of human beings."
— Helen Keller

Research Says...

To become "world-class" in an instrument or sport takes 10,000 hours of practice before the age of 20. The single most important aspect of motivation for world-class performance is the ability to commit to a rigorous practice schedule.

Motivation Questions

What's the difference between motivation and initiative?

Are you more motivated by how you feel or by what you think (to the extent that those are separate)? How about compared to how other people feel/think?

Sometimes people say others "are not living up to their potential" — what does that mean? Is there such a thing as potential, or is it just expectation?

Are you motivated by the same factors that motivate your friends?

Which takes more motivation — to be a "workaholic" or for a "workaholic" to take a break?

Motivation Inspiration

Role Models

Nobel Prize winners have dedicated their lives to solving problems. To read about their work and accomplishments, browse the Nobel website: www.almaz.com

Scott Hamilton is a World Champion ice skater who will continue to skate despite a battle with cancer.

John Wooden was a UCLA coach who inspired hundreds of athletes to give their all. His team had more consecutive winning seasons than any other in the history of college basketball.

Books and Movies For Younger People

 Fly Away Home — a girl sees a problem and does what it takes to solve it. Along the way, she discovers that love is a powerful motivator.

 The Natural — determination creates a second chance for an aging but talented athlete.

 Cool Runnings — a group of runners is so committed to representing their country in the Olympics that they create the first ever Jamaican bob sled team.

Books and Movies For Older People

 Pastwatch: The Redemption of Christopher Columbus, Orson Scott Card — what made Columbus turn westward? How could the outcome have been different? This alternate history weaves the myriad paths of conflict and redemption through the threads of time.

 Chariots of Fire — faith and idealism conflict with politics in this epic saga of runners whose champion their ideals through competition.

 Hoop Dreams — a documentary about two boys growing up in Detroit and reaching for the NBA.

Emotional Intelligence
Courage
Adversity
Perseverance
Interdependence
Empathy
Creativity
Noble Goal
Motivation
Curiosity
Accountability
Optimism
Forgiveness
Initiative
Conflict
Humor
Tolerance
Service
Truth
Tranquility
Awareness
Resiliency
Self-Control
Fusion
Integrity

Curiosity

Curiosity Activities

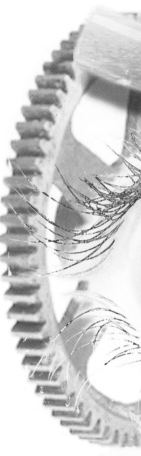

• Ask your children questions to which you do not know the answer.

• Browse in the library in the general reference section for question and answer books, such as *Do Fish Sleep?* by D. Feldman.

• Create a special time, such as after dinner or while driving, to wonder. Wonder if computers really are like brains, wonder how many lemonade stand sales it would take to pay the national debt, wonder how much pollution you would cut if we all rode bikes to work and school once a month. Wondering takes data, but it doesn't matter if you are 100% accurate — approximation is fine. Sometimes books and other tools help wondering, but sometimes that just makes it fussy.

• When you are driving, leave enough time to stop and explore. Read the "historical marker" signs, ask someone about their town, and see where that road leads.

• Suggest to your teacher that it would be fun (and research says valuable) to have time where everyone in class can <u>only</u> ask questions. No answers, no discussion — just questions! When it works well, questions will lead to other questions in a reflective process.

• Look differently. Carry a magnifying glass, borrow a telescope, lay on your back and look up, use a mirror and look backwards. See how the world looks from many perspectives.

Indulging curiosity is a giant banana split for your brain. Your brain is a marvelously capable wonder. Are you curious about all it can do? Set it free and travel the world.

Curiosity is a building block for motivation and reflective thinking. Curiosity helps us get involved; it also helps us consider who and why we are.

Children have a remarkable level of curiosity, but instead of dampening it we need to help them focus it. When you've heard, "Why... why... how come..." 'til you're ready to pop, say, "That's a good question, let's figure it out."

Curiosity Quotes

"To the mind, curiosity is its own reward. And the by-product of perpetual curiosity is wisdom."

— Chip R. Bell

"The world is but a school of inquiry."   — Michel de Montaigne

Research Says...

Questions trigger the brain's thinking processes; there are different kinds of questions, and some engage the brain more thoroughly. There are three general categories of questions: 1) factual (e.g., "What color is Jane's shirt?"); 2) interpretive (e.g., "Why do you think Bob tried to hide?"); and 3) fusion (e.g., "How would you teach Bob to be more responsible?").

Even inane questions lead to thinking, but currently 80-90% of the questions in classrooms, families, and textbooks are at the factual level.

Curiosity Fusion Questions

How far can an airplane fly in the time it takes a butterfly to fly across your city? How much fuel would the airplane use?

If you took a ball-bearing and enlarged it to the size of the earth, would it be rougher or smoother than the planet?

Descartes said, "I think therefore I am." Do you think you would exist without thought?

In how many "languages" do you think? Count spoken languages as well as pictures, music, and symbols.

What is the difference between "curious" and "thoughtful"?

If you have questions in your head, but don't do anything about them (to search for answers), does that mean you are not really curious?

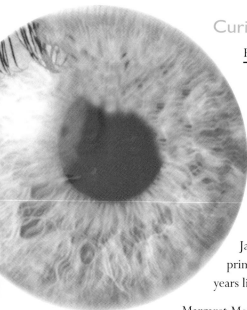

Curiosity Inspiration

Role Models

Tonagawa Susumu is a Japanese molecular biologist who won the 1987 Nobel Prize for immune system research.

Leonardo da Vinci was an artist, scientist, and philosopher who studied all parts of life.

Jane Goodall decided to see how primates really lived, so she spent years living with them.

Margaret Meade studied dozens of human cultures in a relentless inquiry into the nature of culture.

Books and Movies For Younger People

 The Way Things Work, David MacAulay — a visual encyclopedia of the inner workings of human invention.

 The Math Curse, John Scieszka — the world is made of math and there is no way to escape the questions.

 Mrs. Frisbee and the Rats of NIMH, Robert O'Brien — a book and movie about a band of rats trying to find out who they are and where they come from.

Books and Movies For Older People

 Contact, Carl Sagan — Jody Foster plays a scientist in the SETI program whose curiosity impels her to question the most basic assumptions of science.

 Fatman and Little Boy — the struggle of ethics and science that leads to creating the hydrogen bomb.

 Jurassic Park, Michael Crichton — just because we can, does that mean we should?

Emotional Intelligence
Courage
Adversity
Perseverance
Interdependence
Empathy
Creativity
Noble Goal
Motivation
Curiosity
Accountability
Optimism
Forgiveness
Initiative
Conflict
Humor
Tolerance
Service
Truth
Tranquility
Awareness
Resiliency
Self-Control
Fusion
Integrity

Accountability is continuous self-evaluation. It requires a goal, a performance standard, and a timeline.

Accountability includes recognizing and following through on a commitment. The commitment can be to yourself, but most frequently it is to another individual or a group. In fact, accountability is closely tied to interdependence because both require taking care of each other and the group.

Children as young as two can begin to learn the lessons of accountability.

Accountability

Accountability Activities

- Create family "customer response" cards like some restaurants and hotels have to evaluate various aspects of family "performance."

- Create standards for some basic family responsibilities — like cleaning up — that vary depending on need (for instance, dishes can sit in the sink up to 2 hours , but not at all when company is over). Create a system of celebrations and rewards (incentive programs) for when these are met.

- When children (or adults) say, "It is not my fault!" ask, "But what part is your responsibility?"

- Have a family dinner where different people have specific responsibilities. Divide all the responsibilities from different foods to setting the table to hosting. Do not remind anyone of their responsibility; let the event speak for itself.

- Redeem your time. Keep a list of quick tasks that you can do while you are waiting.

- Next time you feel like you are wronged or are a victim, create a list of causes and determine which you could have changed (or still can change!).

- Imagine you were going to hire someone to be you. Write a job description for all the responsibilities that person would have. Prioritize the jobs and identify special skills. Now use the description to evaluate how well you do your "job" of life.

- Someone in your past, maybe a teacher, held you accountable and you learned something critical about yourself and your relationships. Send a postcard to that person and tell them the lesson you learned.

- Create a family investment club with financial goals. Begin with play money, then advance to the real thing. Decide how to distribute accruals, including how much to give away.

> *"It is easier to fight for one's principles than to live up to them"*
>
> — Alfred Adler

Emotional Intelligence
Courage
Adversity
Perseverance
Interdependence
Empathy
Creativity
Noble Goal
Motivation
Curiosity
Accountability
Optimism
Forgiveness
Initiative
Conflict
Humor
Tolerance
Service
Truth
Tranquility
Awareness
Resiliency
Self-Control
Fusion
Integrity

Accountability Quotes

"The man who does things makes many mistakes but he never makes the biggest mistake of all — doing nothing."

— Benjamin Franklin

"Never grow a wishbone... where your backbone ought to be."

— Clementine Paddleford

Research says...

Of 200,000 students surveyed (PRIDE 1995), 33% said that their parents often do not set clear rules. And 50% said that they are not disciplined routinely when they break the rules.

Only 38% of people who make a New Year's resolution have stuck to their plan one week later. After six months, only 15% have managed to hold on to their goals.

Accountability Questions

Do you hold yourself accountable or do other people hold you accountable?

Does law replace accountability? What would happen if no one held her/ himself accountable?

What is the relationship between not holding yourself accountable and being a victim?

How do you know the difference between a mistake and a lack of accountability? What about an accident and accountability? Is there a difference?

What does it mean that the word "accountability" has the word "account" in it?

Can young children teach themselves to be accountable, or do they need older people to teach it? Does it grow "naturally" from experience?

Accountability Inspiration

Role Models

Voltaire — a philosopher and writer whose works attacked injustice.

Simon Wiesenthal — after surviving the Holocaust he worked to reunite families and track down war criminals. The LA Tolerance Museum honors him.

Jocelyn Elders — a US Surgeon General who stood up for her beliefs even when faced with dismissal.

"Every minute starts an hour."
— Paul Gondola

Books and Movies For Younger People

 ET — scientists interfere and nearly kill an outer-space visitor.

 Alexander and the Terrible, Horrible, No Good, Very Bad Day, Judith Viorst — a boy makes himself feel worse by blaming others.

 Free Willy — kids free a suffering animal.

 War Games — a teen's computer hacking almost starts a nuclear war which he and his girlfriend must stop.

Books and Movies For Older People

 Rain Man — in taking responsibility for his autistic brother, a man learns about family and love.

 Man for All Seasons — Sir Thomas Moore refuses to let politics influence his most fundamental beliefs.

 Paper Moon — Tatum and Ryan O'Neil play daughter and father who find out that without accountability there is no stability.

 A Game of Thrones, George Martin — in a world of magical intrigue, the Stark children must decide where loyalty lies.

Emotional Intelligence
Courage
Adversity
Perseverance
Interdependence
Empathy
Creativity
Noble Goal
Motivation
Curiosity
Accountability
Optimism
Forgiveness
Initiative
Conflict
Humor
Tolerance
Service
Truth
Tranquility
Awareness
Resiliency
Self-Control
Fusion
Integrity

Optimism

Optimism is rooted in the knowledge that we have the power to change, grow, and move forward. It is fostered by love and support from others, but its power comes from a deep commitment to self and to reaching out.

Optimists see failure as a transitory obstacle that can be overcome with additional effort. Interestingly, they are right: Ability is not a fixed property; it is highly influenced by hope, self-efficacy, and expectation. People with high optimism are able to motivate themselves when caught in a difficult situation and they make a new path.

"Deep in their roots, all flowers keep the light."

— Theodore Roethke

Emotional Intelligence
Courage
Adversity
Perseverance
Interdependence
Empathy
Creativity
Noble Goal
Motivation
Curiosity
Accountability
Optimism
Forgiveness
Initiative
Conflict
Humor
Tolerance
Service
Truth
Tranquility
Awareness
Resiliency
Self-Control
Fusion
Integrity

Optimism Activities

• Take a child to the hospital where s/he was born and see the newborn section. Help her/him see how much growth has taken place, and talk about the growth yet to come.

• In the story of *Sadako and the Thousand Paper Cranes*, Sadako finds optimism despite the ravages of leukemia. Learn to fold paper cranes and know that when you have made 1000, your life will be different.

• Observe the power of a tiny seed as you plant it and watch it grow.

• Make a batch of chocolate chip cookies and give them away.

• Design a family flag that celebrates the special qualities of individuals in the family. Display the flag at special occasions.

• Make a "dream box" by covering a box with images of hope and love. Put beautiful rocks, seashells, acorns, or other objects in the box whenever something happens that makes you feel good.

• Get in the habit of singing in the car or while you work.

• Create a tradition at home, school, or work where every day someone takes time to tell a joke or funny story.

• Often optimism diminishes because we feel alone or that others can not see our struggles. Give the optimism postcard to a friend, and ask her to send it to you when you need to be reminded of the power of positive thinking.

Research Says...

In a recent study about measuring success, it was discovered that your level of hope is a better indication of college freshman grades than SAT scores.

In another study, optimistic insurance salespeople outsold competitors by 37%.

Optimism Quotes

"Teaching is the greatest act of optimism." — Colleen Wilcox

"There is a way out of every dark mist, over a rainbow trail."
— Navajo song

Optimism Fusion Questions

What's the difference between "optimistic," "hopeful," and "unrealistic"?

If you teach people to be optimistic, don't you just set them up for disappointment?

What is the relationship between resiliency and optimism? Does one lead to the other?

Optimism Inspiration

Role Models

In the 1972 Olympics, Matt Biondi performed poorly in his first two events. Some watchers thought he would "wash out," but others had seen his remarkable optimism. He then won five gold medals in a row.

Oprah Winfrey overcame childhood trauma and now focuses people on responsibility, gratitude, and positive thinking.

Books and Movies For Younger People

Sadako and the Thousand Paper Cranes, Eleanor Coerr — a sad story, which reminds us that even in death, optimism fills us with life (Sadako's monument is shown in the illustration on page 53).

Fortunately, Remy Charlip — an unfolding stream of cliff-hanging situations each of which has an unfortunate side — as well as a fortunate one.

Annie — a Broadway musical about a plucky young orphan who will make everything better tomorrow.

Books and Movies For Older People

Field of Dreams — a man dreams of building a baseball field; "if you build it they will come."

I Know Why the Caged Bird Sings, Maya Angelou — a girl grows up in adversity but maintains hope.

The Power of One, Bryce Courtenay — a boy finds his power from music, love, and generosity.

Joe Versus the Volcano — a movie of possibilities.

Emotional Intelligence
Courage
Adversity
Perseverance
Interdependence
Empathy
Creativity
Noble Goal
Motivation
Curiosity
Accountability
Optimism
Forgiveness
Initiative
Conflict
Humor
Tolerance
Service
Truth
Tranquility
Awareness
Resiliency
Self-Control
Fusion
Integrity

Forgiveness

Given that imperfection and conflict are inherent parts of humanity, forgiving is a vital skill. Until you have forgiven, you are tied to the conflict, locked in the past. The beauty of forgiveness is that, like ripples on the water, it reaches out and out, liberating as it goes.

You can help someone learn forgiveness by sharing the principle that leads you to make this decision. Some forgiveness principles are: "Temper justice with mercy," "Two wrongs don't make a right," and "Forgive us our tres- passes."

We decide if forgiveness is important by observing the way our role models act. Like all kinds of role modeling, what you do is more powerful than what you say — and your actions are observed even when you are not "at your best."

Forgiveness Activities

- Often we don't know if someone *really* has forgiven us. Talk to an elder or younger about how they *know* the feeling of being forgiven. For younger children, create an "I love you signal"; for instance, three hand squeezes means "I love you."

- It is hard to forgive because some part of us feels wounded by someone else's action. Sadly, carrying the hurt keeps the wound from healing. Try helping someone forgive by discussing what can be done to heal the wound.

- To show a younger person why forgiveness is important, put one drop of food coloring in a glass of water to illustrate how holding a grudge can affect our total being. Then try adding a drop of bleach as an example of forgiveness.

- Bedtime forgiveness: Before bed, think of all the people that you need to forgive and then think of all the people that you love. Frequently, these lists are the same. This activity is valuable for people of all ages.

- As you read the paper or hear current events, discuss how forgiveness could play a role in improving the situations.

- Create a forgiveness symbol to remind you and your family about your commitment to forgive. You could make a centerpiece, place mats, napkin rings, a poster, sign, or abstract design.

- When we carry pain, it builds up into a hard, fierce knot. Sometimes we are afraid to let go of it, sometimes we "know" that we are not at fault and our pride makes us hold on. Free yourself from the burden of your hurt. Forgive, and send her or him a card.

Forgiveness

Emotional Intelligence
Courage
Adversity
Perseverance
Interdependence
Empathy
Creativity
Noble Goal
Motivation
Curiosity
Accountability
Optimism
Forgiveness
Initiative
Conflict
Humor
Tolerance
Service
Truth
Tranquility
Awareness
Resiliency
Self-Control
Fusion
Integrity

Forgiveness Quotes

"Anger is a wind which blows out the lamp of the mind."

— Robert Ingersoll

"Forgiveness is the key to action and freedom."   — Hanhan Arendt

"The weak can never forgive. Forgiveness is the attribute of the strong."

— Mahatma Gandhi

Research says...

Two thousand married couples were studied for over two decades in an attempt to discover the key to long-lasting marriages. It was found that the marriage can survive whether the couple argues vigorously or avoids confrontations altogether. Marriages are in serious jeopardy, however, when contempt, criticism, or stonewalling become habitual.

Marriage is not two people who are perfect together, but two imperfect people who are committed to forgiving.

Forgiveness Fusion Questions

Is there such a thing as "forgive and forget"? What saying would work better?

Why do people hold grudges? What do they get out of it?

If two people totally disagree, can they still respect each other?

Forgiveness Inspiration

Role Models

Spiritual leaders like Jesus, Buddha, or Gandhi.

Reginal Denny — truck driver beaten in the LA uprising who quelled anger through his publicly stated forgiveness.

Phan Thi Kim Phuc — In 1972, Kim Phuc was the nine-year-old girl aflame with napalm in a photo that shocked America. In 1997 she brought a message of forgiveness to the Memorial Wall in Washington: "Use pain and sorrow endured in life and turn it into something good."

Books and Movies For Younger People

Bang Bang You're Dead, L. Fitzhugh and S. Scoppettone — the reward of making peace.

The Potato Man, Megan McDonald — a boy, a peddler, a dog, a pomegranate, and kindness.

The Lion King — to grow up, the lion prince must take responsibility for his action and ask forgiveness.

Hook — for the family to reunite, the son must forgive his father.

Books and Movies For Older People

The Leaves in October by Karen Ackerman — after broken promises, a homeless child and her father find the meaning of "home."

Les Miserables, Victor Hugo — ValJean is a criminal whose life is forever changed by forgiveness. In turn, he transforms his life and becomes a source of solace.

The Elephant Man, Christine Sparks — forgiving past hurts and holding onto truth.

Merchant of Venice, Shakespeare — source of the inspiring speech that begins, "The quality of mercy is not strained, it falleth like a gentle rain from heaven."

Emotional
Intelligence

Courage

Adversity

Perseverance

Interdependence

Empathy

Creativity

Noble Goal

Motivation

Curiosity

Accountability

Optimism

Forgiveness

Initiative

Conflict

Humor

Tolerance

Service

Truth

Tranquility

Awareness

Resiliency

Self-Control

Fusion

Integrity

Initiative

Initiative is the self-reliance and energy to undertake new enterprises with an anticipation of successful completion. It is the force which lets us act on principles rather than simply react to circumstances; it is our power to change. Employers, teachers, and family members applaud individuals who do not need to be cajoled into taking care of responsibilities or trying something new.

We use our independent will to make choices, to transcend background or circumstance, and to create a future consonant with our vision. There is a price for these actions — time, money, compromise — and our initiative is the active force that pays the fee.

Ultimately, it is initiative that lets us forge solutions, create compromise, find the "win-win" alternatives, and live out loud.

Initiative Activities

• Play "what if..."

• Start a letter-writing campaign to applaud a success; encourage friends and neighbors to join you.

• Choose a group or family "action of the week (or month)" that addresses a local problem. Actions could be picking up litter, recycling, or planting flower seeds. As often as possible during that week, follow through with the action.

• Establish a monthly "Self-Starter Award" for the family member, student, or colleague who has taken the most initiative in both taking care of responsibilities and going beyond.

• Think of someone who has offended you. What were/are the issues? How does the other person see it? Take the initiative to have a conversation about the situation. Do it in a way that preserves the dignity of the other person, and begin by accepting your own responsibility in the situation. Remember that feelings, opinions, and perceptions are not facts.

• Keep an initiative diary for one month. Record only those events, ideas, or activities upon which you took action.

• Sometimes the challenge of initiative is not knowing what action to take. In that situation, try making a list of 50 possible actions. Brainstorm. Be silly. Then, choose one and try it right away.

• Choose any creation, invention, or discovery about which you care (for example, solar energy, ice cream, or email). Make an imaginary "flow chart" of the origins and actions that might have led to the discovery.

• Internal rewards stimulate initiative, so ask your family, students, or co-workers to each create a list of 10 internal rewards which move them forward (or would help them move forward). Make a list of what you think the others will choose and compare.

• Often initiative is blocked by fear. Create a "super-person" t-shirt or name tag to wear to remind yourself of what it would be like to act without fear. You do not even need to wear it — just hold onto the knowledge that you can, in fact, act in spite of fear.

Emotional Intelligence

Courage

Adversity

Perseverance

Interdependence

Empathy

Creativity

Noble Goal

Motivation

Curiosity

Accountability

Optimism

Forgiveness

Initiative

Conflict

Humor

Tolerance

Service

Truth

Tranquility

Awareness

Resiliency

Self-Control

Fusion

Integrity

Initiative Quotes

"Love is a verb." — Clare Boothe Luce

"Adventure is worthwhile in itself."
— Amelia Earhart

"The ultimate measure of a man is not where he stands in a moment of comfort and convenience, but where he stands at times of challenge and controversy."
— Martin Luther King, Jr.

"He was a bold man that swallowed the first oyster."
— Jonathan Swift

"I knew someone had to take the first step and I made up my mind not to move."
— Rosa Parks

"Action may not always bring happiness, but there is no happiness without action."
— Benjamin Disraeli

Research Says...

William Oncken suggests six levels of initiative: 1) waiting until instructed; 2) asking for permission; 3) recommending; 4) acting and reporting immediately; 5) acting and reporting periodically; and 6) acting independently. Productivity and satisfaction increase as people move toward the sixth level.

Initiative Fusion Questions

Which level of initiative (above) is most like you?

Research says trust is part of initiative — why is that? How would changing trust change your initiative?

What's the difference between initiative to start a job and initiative to finish it?

Initiative Inspiration

Role Models

Thomas Jefferson, Meriwether Lewis, and William Clark spearheaded the most momentous expedition in American history, an adventure filled with "firsts." Read about it in *Undaunted Courage* by Stephen E. Ambrose.

Katherine Graham took over as Editor of the Washington Post following her husband's death, and made the historical decision to expose the Watergate break-in.

César Chavez was a labor organizer who founded the American Farm Workers Association in 1962 and organized produce boycotts when workers were being exploited.

Amelia Bloomer invented bloomers so that women could ride bicycles, fought against unjust marriage laws, and created the first feminist newspaper.

Books and Movies For Younger People

Frindle, Andrew Clements — a boy calls his pen a "frindle" to annoy his 5th grade teacher, and finds that his initiative is rewarded.

Owen, Kevin Henkes — a family must find a creative solution to help Owen go to school.

The Ernest Green Story — a young black student desegregates a southern high school in 1958 and triumphs over the intolerance which bombards him.

Books and Movies For Older People

A Girl Named Disaster, Nancy Farmer — a Shona girl in Mozambique runs away from her oppressive family in a journey of discovery, spirit, identity, and strength.

Not In This Town — homemaker Tammie Schnitzer takes a lonely stand to save her community from hate mongers and ultimately forms the Montana Human Rights Coalition.

Gideon's Trumpet — an indigent prisoner, unjustly convicted without counsel, fights for his right to an attorney and changes US legal history.

Emotional Intelligence

Courage

Adversity

Perseverance

Interdependence

Empathy

Creativity

Noble Goal

Motivation

Curiosity

Accountability

Optimism

Forgiveness

Initiative

Conflict

Humor

Tolerance

Service

Truth

Tranquility

Awareness

Resiliency

Self-Control

Fusion

Integrity

Conflict

Conflict is a fact of life. It is an integral part of interacting with others, and it is a powerful force for growth, clarity, and intentionality. In all the millions of conflicts we experience in our lives, the vast majority end with positive results. Still, because it is uncomfortable, most people want to eliminate or avoid it.

Conflict leads to understanding. It is a clarifier. It provides boundaries and stimulates personal growth. Research demonstrates many positive outcomes of conflict including enriched relationships, ingenuity in solutions, and improved productivity.

Rather than attempting to avoid conflict, learn to creatively manage it and make it a growth experience for all participants.

"After the game,
the king and the pawn
go into the same box."
— Italian proverb

the rock & the rive

Conflict Activities

Emotional
Intelligence

Courage

Adversity

Perseverance

Interdependence

Empathy

Creativity

Noble Goal

Motivation

Curiosity

Accountability

Optimism

Forgiveness

Initiative

Conflict

Humor

Tolerance

Service

Truth

Tranquility

Awareness

Resiliency

Self-Control

Fusion

Integrity

- Usually conflict turns negative when we fall into a pattern of unthinking behavior. Try making a chart or graph that shows how your conflicts usually flow.

- Think of your last argument. List ten actions or statements the other person could have done/said that would have made you feel resolution.

- When you need to confront someone, first list three choices of how to bring up the issue.

- For a month, keep a conflict record in your journal or diary. List the people and issues with which you've had conflict. For each, make sure to write the **positive** outcome — the lessons learned, the closer relationships, or the personal growth. As you add to your record, keep reviewing the data in order to recognize patterns. What will you do differently next time?

- Or, try this journal activity: For a week list all the conflicts you see on tv, in literature, and in life. For each, include descriptions of the people, the conflict, and the result. Look for patterns; what are the topics of conflict? Do younger, older, male, or female characters act differently in conflicts?

- People tend to follow ingrained patterns in conflict. Next time, experiment with the opposite of your usual response. If you usually get quiet, try speaking more assertively; if you usually apologize, try sticking it out longer and working for a compromise.

- Help a youngster make a picture book about a child who has a disagreement with her friends or family. Encourage her to choose a topic about which she rebels, such as not wanting to take a bath. In the picture book, create three different possibilities of what could happen to resolve the issue.

- Fold a paper in quarters. In the top left write "people, dislike"; in the lower left, write "places, dislike"; on the top right, "people, like"; and the bottom right, "places, like." Fill in the chart, then imagine mixing one like with one dislike. What happens if you take a "person, like" and see them in a "place, dislike"? This technique can help show that feelings can be flexible.

Conflict Quotes

"If we could read the secret history of our enemies, we should find in each man's life such sorrow and suffering enough to disarm all hostility."
— Henry Wadsworth Longfellow

"I learned long ago never to wrestle a pig. You get dirty, and besides, the pig likes it."
— Cyrus Ching

"There are some things you learn best in calm, and some in storm."
— Willa Cather

"The world is wide, I will not waste my life in friction when it could be turned into momentum."
— Frances Willard

Research Says...

Women are perceived as being less credible and less effective in attempting to resolve tension when they use "self-trivializing messages." These include rising tone of voice, qualifiers, disclaimers, and tag questions (e.g., saying, "This will not work," then tagging on, "Will it?").

There are at least five levels of conflict: 1) problem to solve; 2) problem plus difficult relationship; 3) problem escalates to "right" vs. "wrong" sides with others enlisted to support each side; 4) conflict appears to have a "life of its own"; and 5) conflict plus desire to hurt, banish, or destroy others. Understanding the level makes it easier to solve the conflict by using appropriate tools.

Conflict Fusion Questions

What is a "typical" response to conflict? What is yours (run, shout, listen...)?

After some conflicts, the opposing people feel closer together; sometimes they feel farther apart — what makes that happen?

Why do people who love one another argue?

Conflict Inspiration

Role Models

Elie Wiesel — Nazi concentration camp survivor and 1986 Nobel Peace Prize winner dedicated to preserving the memory of the Holocaust.

Vaclav Havel — revolutionary poet and Czech president who believes that true power comes from the voices of those who act together and in conscience.

Janet Reno — US Attorney General who facilitates positive conflict by taking responsibility for her decisions.

Books and Movies For Younger People

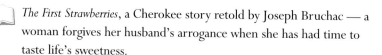

The First Strawberries, a Cherokee story retold by Joseph Bruchac — a woman forgives her husband's arrogance when she has had time to taste life's sweetness.

Don't Fidget a Feather, Erica Silverman — through a friendly contest, a duck and a gander discover that everyone has strengths.

Zelda and Ivy, Laura Kvasnosky — sibling rivalry, sibling love.

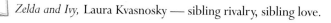

Where the Red Fern Grows, Wilson Rawls — a heart-wrenching story of the mutual love between a boy and his dogs.

Books and Movies For Older People

Verbal Judo: The Gentle Art of Persuasion, George J. Johnson, English professor and martial arts master — defines a philosophy that allows you to respond rather than react and face everyday arguments with a plan to engage people through empathy.

On Golden Pond (PG) — conflict among three generations.

The Turning Point (PG) — friendship and rivalry between two women; pent up bitterness and disappointment over life choices and paths not taken explodes into an outpouring of emotion.

The Dubious Hills, Pamela Dean — when wizards created this land, they eliminated conflict, but they also limited human potential.

Emotional
Intelligence

Courage

Adversity

Perseverance

Interdependence

Empathy

Creativity

Noble Goal

Motivation

Curiosity

Accountability

Optimism

Forgiveness

Initiative

Conflict

Humor

Tolerance

Service

Truth

Tranquility

Awareness

Resiliency

Self-Control

Fusion

Integrity

"Laughter is the shortest distance between two people."

Victor Borg

Humor unleashes your mind. It is a complex interpersonal dynamic with many sources. At times, humor comes from clarity — we see a comic strip or we hear a joke that reminds us of our actions, and we laugh at ourselves.

Laughter has positive emotional, physical, and cognitive effects. It is a fantastic stress reducer. It reduces inflammation as measured by the sedimentation rate. It stimulates imagination, creativity, and problem solving skills. Laughter helps people think more broadly and associate more freely so they notice connections that may have eluded them otherwise. This kind of association is critical both to making decisions and to understanding consequences.

Humor is mental flexibility. It is essential to sanity and survival, it is a tonic for loneliness and depression, and it is the foundation of positive social interaction.

Humor

Humor Activities

• Cut out words and sentences from newspapers/magazines and rearrange them into a funny story. Illustrate your piece with cutout pictures/cartoons.

• Commit to adding humor to your life. Each week, read one humorous book, attend one comedy event, or tell seven jokes. Share what makes you laugh with at least one person, and record them in the "brain ticklers" section of your journal.

• Invent a tongue-twister.

• Pick a limerick, rhyme, or song and make a new version. For example, instead of a little lamb, "Mary had a parrot, It talked to her all day. Between them both, They said so much, There's nothing more to say." Send your creation to Six Seconds.

• When working on a project, think of ways to do it "all wrong" that would make you laugh.

• Make a set of cards each listing unusual items such as cattails, inner tubes, chain link fences, porcupines, or cotton candy. Play a game where each person or team picks a card, then has five minutes to think of as many alternative uses as possible.

• The egg is the subject of more riddles around the world than any other item. Here's an example: "I have a barrel, thin as thin, with two kinds of water in." Make up your own, and send them to Six Seconds.

• Collect cartoons or jokes that remind you of each member of your family, class, or work team. Have a special celebration and exchange jokes.

• Play "spoon hockey" on the table with spoons and a small foam ball or an object from the "junk drawer." Find other unusual materials and make up variations on the game.

Emotional Intelligence

Courage

Adversity

Perseverance

Interdependence

Empathy

Creativity

Noble Goal

Motivation

Curiosity

Accountability

Optimism

Forgiveness

Initiative

Conflict

Humor

Tolerance

Service

Truth

Tranquility

Awareness

Resiliency

Self-Control

Fusion

Integrity

Humor Quotes

"Humor teaches tolerance."   — W. Somerset Maugham

"He deserves paradise, who makes his companions laugh."
                                                — The Koran

"Laughter can be more satisfying than honor; more precious than money."
                                                — Harriet Rochlin

*"I had rather have a fool to make me
merry than experience to make me sad."*
                    — William Shakespeare

Research Says...

Children laugh an average of
200 times per day, and adults an
average of 17.

Cousins reports many physical
effects from laughter. Ten
minutes of "belly laughter" can
provide two hours of pain-free sleep.
Laughter also is a factor in recovering from disease. It reduces inflammation,
enhances breathing, and increases the production of immune cells.

Humor Fusion Questions

How much do you laugh each day? Why would adults usually laugh so much
less than do children?

What would people be like with no sense of humor? Like Dr. Spock from
Star Trek, or different? How?

Does the sound of people's laughter say something about their personalities?
What?

Do you learn "serious" ideas better by being serious or by laughing? Why?

Sometimes people laugh when they are overwhelmed or confused — what's
the difference between that and "funny" laughter? Why does it happen?

Humor Inspiration

Emotional
Intelligence

Courage

Adversity

Perseverance

Interdependence

Empathy

Creativity

Noble Goal

Motivation

Curiosity

Accountability

Optimism

Forgiveness

Initiative

Conflict

Humor

Tolerance

Service

Truth

Tranquility

Awareness

Resiliency

Self-Control

Fusion

Integrity

Role Models

Matt Groening — the creator of *Life Is Hell* and *The Simpsons* whose humor provokes, challenges, and tests as it amuses.

Norman Lear — creator of the ground-breaking, irreverent sitcom, *All In The Family,* which was a mirror that allowed a nation to look inside and see the bigot within each of us.

Bob Hope spent every December for over 40 years away from his family in order to bring humor and appreciation to servicemen stationed overseas during the holidays.

Bailey White, Garrison Keilor, and Daniel Pinkwater are all authors and NPR personalities who teach us through laughter.

Books and Movies For Younger People

Good Night Gorilla, Peggy Rathmann — a humorous bedtime story about the zoo.

Squashed, Joan Bauer — a teenage girl, a giant pumpkin, and the thrill of competition.

Books and Movies For Older People

Daisy Faye and The Miracle Man, Fannie Flagg — a girl from a unique family and her hilarious adventures of growing up.

Growing Up, Russell Baker — beautifully written memoir of an extraordinary "ordinary childhood" touchingly recalled through the prism of humor.

Divine Secrets of the Ya-Ya Sisterhood, Rebecca Wells — entertaining and insightful intergenerational novel about the complex bonds between mother and daughter.

Sleeping at the Starlite Motel, Bailey White — wit and wisdom, truth and surprise, an astounding adventure into the foibles of life.

The Princess Bride (PG) — a hilarious tale of wit and whimsey that will unlock your imagination and inspire your dreams.

Tolerance

Tolerance is a doorway to acceptance. It depends on a recognition that difference is not wrong, that your experience is not universal, and that together we are greater than the sum of our parts.

Tolerance comes from recognizing sameness — or that similarities outweigh differences. We all have common needs and many common beliefs — it is just the details that are different. It is easy, for example, to agree about the significance of peace, yet difficult to make decisions about the placement of fences.

Many nations have passed strict laws to mitigate ethnic discrimination, but the laws do not eliminate personal bias. Racism ends in families, neighborhoods, and communities. It ends when we recognize it within ourselves, and when we take responsibility for changing our own beliefs and actions.

Tolerance Activities

Emotional
Intelligence

Courage

Adversity

Perseverance

Interdependence

Empathy

Creativity

Noble Goal

Motivation

Curiosity

Accountability

Optimism

Forgiveness

Initiative

Conflict

Humor

Tolerance

Service

Truth

Tranquility

Awareness

Resiliency

Self-Control

Fusion

Integrity

• Usually we are intolerant due to lack of understanding, information, or knowledge. Pick someone or something that bugs you, that "gets under your skin." Learn all you can about him, her, or it.

• Make a list of the characteristics that incorporate tolerance (i.e., compassion, empathy, suspension of judgment, insight...). Rank yourself on each characteristic, then choose one to practice.

• Think of a time when you felt uncomfortable. What one thing could someone have said or done to make you feel more at ease? Find opportunities to empathize with others who look uncomfortable, and do that one thing for them.

• Describe someone you "hate." Make a detailed list, and put it aside for a few days, weeks, or even months. When you look at the list again, see how many of those words also describe you.

• Intolerance flourishes through stereotypes. Pick a stereotype, and then find someone from that group. How many attributes of the stereotype fit that person? What are the stereotypes that others might apply to you? How accurate are they?

• In dealing with stereotypes, people often assume that their friend is the "exception to the rule." What happens if you assume every positive aspect of people that you know is applicable to every person in their "group"?

• Become a "keypal" (email penpal) with someone from another country. If you are a teacher, have your classroom correspond with a classroom across the world (many nations have lists of "schools on the internet" — write to the "postmaster" at a school and ask to be put in touch with a teacher of your grade level/subject area).

• Make a list of everything you know or think about a culture. Then visit a museum, read books, see documentaries, study the culture in depth. Where did the stereotypes arise? How accurate were you?

• List as many proverbs/clichés about tolerance as you can (e.g., "People who live in glass houses..."; "You can't judge a book..."; "What goes around..."). Why are these proverbs so common? Have you used them? When should people use them?

Tolerance Quotes

"The highest result of education is tolerance." — Helen Keller

"You can never be what you ought to be until I am what I ought to be."
— Martin Luther King, Jr.

"We are more alike, my friend, than we are unalike." — Maya Angelou

"Unless we live what we know, we do not even know it." — Thomas Menton

"The whole world watches to see whether the democratic ideal in human relationships is viable." — Gordon Allport

"Ultimately, whoever hates, hates his brother. And when he hates his brother, he hates himself." — Elie Weisel

Research Says...

German men who resisted the Nazis had mothers who were highly "demonstrative" and provided a "sense of early and basic security" (Allport).

A similar study of non-Jews who helped Jews escape found that "rescuers" had close relationships with mother/father and saw other people as "basically good." Children from homes that are warm, nurturing, and loving tend to view others (and the larger community) as a similar place.
Despite differences in child-rearing practices across cultures, love is the essential ingredient in building tolerance.

Tolerance Fusion Questions

If you like someone or find them attractive, are you more tolerant? Why?

How do you know if your response is your own belief instead of one from your society or family?

What is the difference between tolerance and acceptance? Is tolerance "good enough," or does equality only come from acceptance? How do you move from one to the other?

Should you be tolerant of intolerance? Of hate?

Does tolerance lead to *more* tolerance?

Can you legislate tolerance?

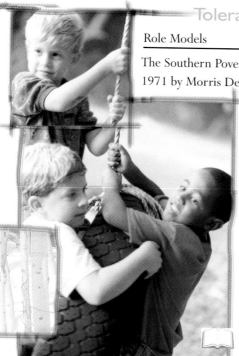

Tolerance Inspiration

Role Models

The Southern Poverty Law Center was founded in 1971 by Morris Dees "To combat hate, intolerance and discrimination through education and litigation." Their biannual Teaching Tolerance magazine is an outstanding resource (www.splcenter.org).

Whitney Young — American civil rights leader, executive director of National Urban League from 1961-1971.

Books and Movies For Younger People

 All the Colors of the Earth, Sheila Hamanaka — finding strength in difference.

 Beauty and the Beast, Disney — in this classic tale, love overcomes differences and creates redemption.

 The Great Ball Game, a Muskogee story retold by Joseph Bruchac — the animals and birds compete, but the outcast bat wins the day.

Chester's Way, Kevin Henkes — when new friends move to town, it takes some tolerance to make a place for them.

Books and Movies For Older People

 Journey of the Sparrows, Fran Buss — a moving epic of a poor illegal immigrant girl facing loneliness, loss, and looking for hope.

 Once Upon A Time When We Were Black — the love and kinship of a tight-knit community provides the encouragement to overcome bigotry and intolerance in the segregated South.

Orbital Resonance, John Barnes — to save the earth, the residents of an asteroid ship engineer a new society, and their children must either fit in or take over.

Emotional Intelligence
Courage
Adversity
Perseverance
Interdependence
Empathy
Creativity
Noble Goal
Motivation
Curiosity
Accountability
Optimism
Forgiveness
Initiative
Conflict
Humor
Tolerance
Service
Truth
Tranquility
Awareness
Resiliency
Self-Control
Fusion
Integrity

Service

Service makes us more human. It is the antidote to depression — and the more anonymous the gift, the more powerful the antidote. Service promotes the mental and emotional health of the giver — it provides happiness, joy, and a sense of efficacy. True service also builds community and a sense of connection.

We need to realize that giving/taking is a cycle in life. At times we will be givers — at times, receivers. We should learn to receive in a thoughtful, kind, accepting way that will help the giver grow. We should give in a respectful, humble way that recognizes that we are getting as much as we are giving.

Service provides the opportunity to make a significant difference in the neighborhood, community, nation, or world. Depending on your interest and commitment, you can clean up the air, decrease neighborhood violence, save the rainforests, combat drug abuse, or add to world peace. Speak up! Speak out! Design the world in which you want to live.

Service Activities

• Pick a problem in your community that needs work. Begin with some basic research: What are the needs? Who is involved? What forces/people are in opposition? Who will be allies? Then pick one of those allies and begin!

• Write a press release or a letter to the editor identifying an issue, your goals, and rationale for the action you are taking. Tell people how they can get involved.

• Contact the state or federal legislator for your area about your project. Let them know about your work and tell them what they could do to help — or even what laws they could write in this matter.

• Register to adopt a guide-dog puppy for the years before training begins. Or, adopt one who is retired and provide the dog with the love, nurture, and care deserved after all those years of service.

• Find individuals in your community who need tutoring or mentoring. Share your special skills and interests, offer to be a reading mentor at the children's library, or volunteer to help with after-school supervision at a local school.

• Contribute time to a senior center, a Boys and Girls Club, a YMCA, a charitable organization, a church/synagogue/mosque/temple, or a shelter. When you volunteer, find out what help is most needed.

• With a group of people from school or work, clean up a park, beach, stream, or other area. Ask the authorities if you can plant flowers or do other projects to help beautify the area.

• Adopt a military unit stationed overseas and send a letter every month. You can ask your local recruiting office to help you connect with women and men from your area.

• Bring treats, flowers, cards, etc. to someone in the neighborhood. If you are doing this with your child, don't assume s/he will "get it" just by watching — tell her/him about what you are doing and why.

• Make a list of everyone whose service and work contributes to your school or other organization. See if you can list every single person — including those who might not even know of their support.

Emotional
Intelligence

Courage

Adversity

Perseverance

Interdependence

Empathy

Creativity

Noble Goal

Motivation

Curiosity

Accountability

Optimism

Forgiveness

Initiative

Conflict

Humor

Tolerance

Service

Truth

Tranquility

Awareness

Resiliency

Self-Control

Fusion

Integrity

Service Quotes

"Many persons have the wrong idea of what constitutes true happiness. It is not attained through self-gratification but through fidelity to a worthy purpose."

— Helen Keller

"One thing I know: the only ones among you who will be really happy are those who will have sought and found how to serve."

— Albert Schweitzer

"Make yourself necessary to somebody." — Ralph Waldo Emerson

"Now the trumpet summons us again — not as a call to bear arms, though arms we need — not as a call to battle, though embattled we are — but a call to bear the burden of a long twilight struggle, year in and year out, "rejoicing in hope, patient in tribulation" — a struggle against the enemies of man: tyranny, poverty, disease, and war itself."

— John F. Kennedy

Research Says...

In the US, 13 million teens volunteer an average of 3.9 hours per week. In 1995, Americans did 20.3 billion hours of service. Each year, the average American household contributes $1000 to charity.

Service Questions

How much time did you spend last month helping others? To what would you like to make a greater contribution?

When you have helped someone, what feelings were generated? What can you do to spread those?

What prevents people from giving more service?

Research says that if you give **anonymously**, the positive emotional benefits are greater. Why is that?

Service Inspiration

Role Models

Thich Nhat Hanh, a Vietnamese Buddhist monk ordained at 16, adapts ancient teachings to modern problems through his writings and lectures on mindful living and social responsibility. In 1964 he founded the *School of Youth for Social Service,* the "little Peace Corps."

Eunice Kennedy Shriver founded the *Special Olympics* in the 1960s. The organization now serves over a million athletes in nearly 150 countries (www.specialolympics.org).

Clinton Hill founded *Kids for Saving the Earth* when he was 10, shortly before he died of a brain tumor. The organization now has 30,000 members (612-559-0602).

Dorothea Dix, horrified by the plight of the mentally ill in 1843, was a catalyst for new hospital treatment programs in 16 states.

Books and Movies For Younger People

Kate Shelley and the Midnight Express, M. K. Wetterer — the true story of a girl who overcomes her fears to save a train full of people.

Clown of God, Tomie de Paola — when an old juggler gives the only gift he has, people are influenced by the miracle which happens.

50 Simple Things Kids Can Do To Save The Earth, Earth Works Group.

The Rag Coat by Lauren Mills — friends provide the warmth of love when they make a rag coat for a classmate to wear to school in winter.

All Dogs Go To Heaven — a touching tale of a tough old dog who becomes the guardian of a young orphan.

Books and Movies For Older People

And the Band Played On — In the summer of 1981, a handful of strong-willed men and women take on an indifferent nation. They seek the key to several mysterious deaths from the yet undiscovered AIDS virus.

Leading Lady, Betty White — a guide dog's story of devoted service.

The Memory of Earth, Orson Scott Card — on a foreign world in the far future, a computer reaches out to help man reach his destiny, though change is fraught with peril.

Emotional
Intelligence
Courage
Adversity
Perseverance
Interdependence
Empathy
Creativity
Noble Goal
Motivation
Curiosity
Accountability
Optimism
Forgiveness
Initiative
Conflict
Humor
Tolerance
Service
Truth
Tranquility
Awareness
Resiliency
Self-Control
Fusion
Integrity

Truth

"Truth is something which cannot be told in a few words, and those who simplify the universe only reduce the expansion of its meaning.
—Anaïs Nin

Truth is tied to infinity; it is tested by time. Human theories are in a constant state of flux and vary with each new discovery, each new age. While it would be useful to know what is true and what is not, it rarely happens. In fact, external truth — truth outside of one's own self, or "capital T" Truth — is not visible in single moments. Instead, we approximate it with our most careful perception reflected against our most careful thinking. The internal truth becomes a standard by which we measure external truth, but they are not necessarily the same.

In EQ terms, the first challenge is to recognize the truth of your own emotions. What do you really feel? What does your gut tell you? This internal truth is a powerful guiding force. Sadly, under a torrent of conflicting words, many of us stop listening to our inner voices and truth fades. Through the combined power of heart and mind, however, you can learn to hear yourself more clearly.

The second challenge is to accept that other people will have different truths. We can have astoundingly strong beliefs — but **Truth** is more complex than one person's opinion.

Truth Activities

Emotional
Intelligence

Courage

Adversity

Perseverance

Interdependence

Empathy

Creativity

Noble Goal

Motivation

Curiosity

Accountability

Optimism

Forgiveness

Initiative

Conflict

Humor

Tolerance

Service

Truth

Tranquility

Awareness

Resiliency

Self-Control

Fusion

Integrity

- Pick any subject in which you are interested, and research what people said about that topic a long time ago. See if you can find the "flat earth" beliefs about your topic. Now imagine what people will say about contemporary ideas in 500 years!

- Set a goal of discussing one new fact per day for an entire month. What are the opinions generated about each fact? Make a book with facts on one side and opinions on the opposite. Can you always tell one from another?

- Play "Truth or Dare." Discuss why that game has continued to intrigue generations.

- Identify "truths" from another culture that are in conflict with "truths" from your culture. What created such differences? Can it be "right" that both truths exist? Is one false?

- Collect newspapers from several countries for one day, read about a major international event, and compare the "truth" as reported in the different papers.

- After a group event (e.g., party, field trip, family outing, performance), have each person write or record a detailed chronicle. After 21 days, without reviewing earlier depiction, reconstruct the description from memory. Compare all the versions.

- Pick a word that you commonly use. Look it up in the dictionary and compare the definition with the way you understand the word. Which is right?

- Descartes wrote "I think, therefore I am" after systematically eliminating all "truths" that he could not **prove** to be true. Make a list of things you consider to be true, then sort them into categories: "true no matter what," "true given my own experience," "true given what I've learned or heard." If you found all except the "true no matter what" to be *not* really true, how would that change your life?

- Pick a photograph or painting of an event and compare what the images show with a written explanation. Are the depictions different? Is your interpretation of each depiction different?

Truth Quotes

"I am not afraid of storms for I am learning how to sail my ship." — Louisa May Alcott

"I think and think for months and years. Ninety-nine times, the conclusion is false. The hundredth time I am right." — Albert Einstein

"Many a time I have wanted to stop talking and find out what I really believed." — Walter Lippmann

"Between whom there is hearty truth, there is love."
— Henry David Thoreau

Research Says...

A study of freshman psychology students revealed that episodic memory is weaker than previously believed. Students were asked to describe details of their lives during the dramatic Challenger incident. Three years later, they were asked to recall these experiences. When compared with the original journals, only 10% had correctly recalled key major events; 65% had memories partially correct; 25% were wrong on every major fact.

We accurately remember about one fact out of every 100.

Truth Fusion Questions

If memories are not accurate, are they still truthful?

If someone has an emotion based on "false" information, does that change the truth of the emotion?

To what extent can a fictional story be "true"?

If you were required to testify in court, how would you ensure that you did, indeed, tell the truth, the whole truth, and nothing but the truth?

Religious or "higher" truth aside, if human truth is personal or subjective, what does that suggest?

Truth Inspiration

Role Models

Mother Cabrini's vision, her inner truth, was so strong that she founded the Sacred Heart sisterhood and was cannonized.

Rabbi Marc Gellman and Msgr. Thomas Hartman host a nationally syndicated tv show which helps children understand that God is the same, whatever your religion.

Greg Louganis, Olympic Gold Medal diver, came to terms with overwhelming personal turmoil to make public his homosexuality after a head wound during the Seoul Olympics put his doctors at risk. He wrote his story, *Breaking the Surface*, to share these lessons.

Books and Movies For Younger People

A Day's Work, Eve Bunting — struggling to find work for his grandfather, Francisco lies and eventually learns that truth is more important than money.

Old Turtle, Douglas Wood & Cheng-Khee Chee — a beautifully illustrated fable that speaks to environmental healing and international understanding.

Fairy Tale — a true story of two young girls whose photographs of tiny winged beings are challenged. Are they real or trickery?

Courtney, John Burningham — sans pedigree, a homely mongrel reminds us to look beneath the surface and not make judgments based on appearance.

Books and Movies For Older People

Dangerous Skies, Suzanne Staples — in a poor rural Southern town, a girl is accused of murder and no one defends her. She must find how much she can push for truth when she is isolated and unsupported.

100 Years of Solitude, Gabriel Garcia Marquez — "a sense of all that is profound, meaningful, and meaningless" in the human experience from post Genesis through the air age with wit, wisdom, and poetry.

Class Action (PG-13) — pursuing the truth may endanger the father-daughter relationship of two high-powered attorneys.

Emotional Intelligence · Courage · Adversity · Perseverance · Interdependence · Empathy · Creativity · Noble Goal · Motivation · Curiosity · Accountability · Optimism · Forgiveness · Initiative · Conflict · Humor · Tolerance · Service · **Truth** · Tranquility · Awareness · Resiliency · Self-Control · Fusion · Integrity

Tranquility

Tranquility comes from the joyful application of our principles — it is the result of our inner self being reflected in our actions. This agreement brings peace of conscience, peace of mind, and peace of heart. The loss of tranquility comes from unmet expectations. But does the turmoil come from veering away from those inner guiding principles or from giving too much weight to external voices? Tranquility will grow if you answer with neither pessimism nor a sense of scarcity.

In the Ryonji temple in Kyoto there is a fountain that translates as, "Contentment only exists from learning." It is a reminder that the tranquility comes from "active peace" — that elusive state when we are fully aware and fully open. Tranquility is calm, but it is not drowsy.

"We carry within us the wonders we seek without us."

— Sir Thomas Browne

Tranquility Activities

• Meditation is used all over the world to create tranquility. You can meditate a zillion different ways; one is to imagine your mind like a mirror. You are not ignoring everything around you, but you are not getting caught up in it either.

• Navigators used to know their location based on the North Star. Establish a guiding star for yourself — and then see if your daily actions bring you closer to the star. For one day, try doing **only** those things that are guided by your star. Does that bring tranquility?

• Before you get up in the morning, imagine what needs to happen in your day to build tranquility. Take a few moments of wakeful calm.

• Remember Aesop's fable of the hare and the tortoise? Some of us are rabbits, some turtles. Stress is created when we attempt to be what we are not. Have each family member, student, or co-worker choose an animal each most represents. What characteristics of the animal do they embrace or want to emulate?

• Identify something you do not like about your physical appearance. Stand in front of a mirror, and for six minutes, actively accept that characteristic as positive. Is your mind resistant? Is the resistance from **you** or from messages you've heard?

• Count the number of different thoughts your brain entertains during a three minute span. What did you learn about yourself?

• Self-forgiveness brings tranquility. Identify one of your actions or behaviors toward another person for which you have not forgiven yourself. Think of a way to make restitution. If the other person is not available, find a substitute (i.e., we are all waves in the same ocean).

• Pick a photo or painting which symbolizes tranquility. Put it someplace where you will see it when you need to be reminded of that quality (e.g., binder, desk, kitchen).

• Zen belief holds that by doing something (e.g., raking a garden, making a bowl) with total mindfulness, we can achieve harmony. Next time you have a "mundane" task such as mowing the lawn or washing windows, see if you can give 100% of your mind to that action. Dwell fully in the act.

Emotional
Intelligence

Courage

Adversity

Perseverance

Interdependence

Empathy

Creativity

Noble Goal

Motivation

Curiosity

Accountability

Optimism

Forgiveness

Initiative

Conflict

Humor

Tolerance

Service

Truth

Tranquility

Awareness

Resiliency

Self-Control

Fusion

Integrity

Tranquility Quotes

"Dreams are illustrations from the book your soul is writing about you."
— Marsha Norman

"Still, there is a calm, pure harmony, and music inside of me."
— Vincent van Gough

"When it is dark enough, you can see the stars."   — Charles Beard

"Men are not worried by things that happen, but by their thoughts about those things."
— Epictetus

Research Says...

In a study at Stanford, members of one group were given a lecture on positive attitudes. The second group was taught to relax every muscle in the body — from eyebrows to toes. Both groups then took an achievement test. The "relaxation" group scored 25% higher than the other group.

Tranquility Fusion Questions

Zen koan are "impossible" questions such as, "What was your face before you were born?" or "What is the sound of one hand clapping?" Why do these questions teach tranquility? What else do they teach?

Are you concerned with the ways people evaluate your looks or words? What is the effect of this concern on tranquility? What is the effect of the effect?

People often describe water as "tranquil," yet it is full of motion and life. Why is it tranquil?

Some people take drugs like alcohol or marijuana to create tranquility. What is the difference between "induced" and "natural" tranquility?

Which shows more tranquility — an eagle or an owl?

Tranquility Inspiration

Role Models

Abigail Adams, wife and advisor to President Samuel Adams, was greatly respected for her calm demeanor, exceptional intellect, and insight on national issues.

Kofi Annan is the current Secretary General of the United Nations. His leadership is characterized by gracious diplomacy and respectful, forceful calm that preserves the dignity of the political process.

Books and Movies For Younger People

The Secret Garden, Frances Hodgson Burnett — when Mary finds the hidden garden, she discovers a connection to the past and a solace.

Northern Lullaby, Nancy White Carlstrom — lyrical watercolors and words wrap the reader in the serenity of a snowy Alaskan evening.

Peach and Blue, Sarah Kilborne — as a frog and a peach become friends, they learn to appreciate all that is around them.

Books and Movies For Older People

Hope for the Flowers, Trina Paulus — which is real success, to climb high or to become a butterfly?

The Three Minute Meditator, David Harp — an inspirational and practical guide.

The Blue Jay's Dance, Louise Erdrich — with time stilled by pregnancy, a woman learns to see the world slowly changing.

The Island, Gary Paulsen — a stirring story of a teen boy who finds an island where he has the peace to discover his world and himself.

Hope Floats — finding tranquility from love and family despite the challenges of conflict and adversity.

Emotional Intelligence
Courage
Adversity
Perseverance
Interdependence
Empathy
Creativity
Noble Goal
Motivation
Curiosity
Accountability
Optimism
Forgiveness
Initiative
Conflict
Humor
Tolerance
Service
Truth
Tranquility
Awareness
Resiliency
Self-Control
Fusion
Integrity

Awareness

We live in a rainbow of life. All around us are people with lives of great beauty and stunning complexity. It is literally more than we can absorb. Yet the more we isolate ourselves, the more shallow our own lives become.

Awareness is the capacity to stand apart from ourselves and examine our thinking, our intentions, our behaviors, and our effects on what is around us. It is the ability to turn our "reading glasses" inward upon ourselves.

Awareness includes recognizing our own thoughts, feelings, and actions. How do we respond? What are we really saying? As we learn to recognize and accept our relationship to the large and complex world, we accept more and more responsibility for the consequences of our actions — and even of our thoughts.

"Where there is great love there are always miracles.

— Willa Cathe

Awareness Activities

• Observe your own behaviors for one day. Notice how different situations dictate/influence your behavior; name each of your "characters" and see if you can tell what prompts each "self" to act the way s/he does.

• Next time you are in a restaurant, notice how aware people are of those around them. See if you can tell when someone notices the waitperson coming to help them. Do people notice you watching?

• Videotape yourself doing something routine — like working at your desk or cooking a meal. When you watch the tape you might be embarrassed, so watch it a second time later and observe all your behaviors — how many did you not even notice doing?

• Read *If you Give a Mouse a Cookie* with a child, then create a book or poster of a story of a child's own conflict and its consequences (for example, "If Bobby Wakes Up Late..."). Next time "Bobby" starts on that pattern, ask him/her if today is going to be like the story/poster.

• Create a "mind map" or a pie chart that shows how much energy you put in the different aspects of your life. What could you eliminate? What could you emphasize?

• Dump out the contents of your pockets, wallet, purse, bag; sort them into "past," "present," and "future." If a stranger were to look at these items, what might s/he conclude? Is this who you really are?

• Look at the covers of the magazines displayed in a store. As a group, what do the magazines say about our society?

• Listen to the tone of your voice at different times of day. Are there situations where your voice changes? Why is that?

• Imagine three "magical mystery boxes" in three sizes — tiny, medium, and gigantic. What does each contain? Are the contents tangible? Intangible? What might they contain for a friend or significant other? For children? Why might the contents differ?

• Write down fifty words to describe yourself, then put a star by the most significant descriptions. Ask several people to do the same about you. Compare lists. Usually they are quite different — why is that?

Emotional
Intelligence
Courage
Adversity
Perseverance
Interdependence
Empathy
Creativity
Noble Goal
Motivation
Curiosity
Accountability
Optimism
Forgiveness
Initiative
Conflict
Humor
Tolerance
Service
Truth
Tranquility
Awareness
Resiliency
Self-Control
Fusion
Integrity

Awareness Quotes

"The need for change bulldozed a road down the center of my mind." — Maya Angelou

"I learned to make my mind large, as the universe is large, so there is room for paradoxes." — Maxine Hong Kingston

"We live in a rainbow of chaos." — Paul Cezanne

"Problems are messages." —Shakti Gawain

"Why is life so tragic; so like a little strip of pavement over an abyss. I look down; I feel giddy; I wonder how I am ever to walk to the end." — Virginia Woolf

"It is well to remember that the entire population of the universe, with one trifling exception, is composed of others." — John Andrew Holmes

Research Says...

We always actually focus on only one source at a given time. When it seems like we have a broader focus or appears that we are multi-tasking, we are actually alternating attention back and forth at near the speed of light.

In fact, people can "focus" for less than 30% of the time. For parents and teachers, this means rethinking much of the way we present information. The brain responds to contrasts in emotion, content, or novelty. So, to increase "attention" we actually have to increase variation.

Awareness Fusion Questions

After a short (two minute) break, what happens to your ability to focus?

If you increased your awareness of others, would that change your awareness of yourself? Vice-versa?

Research says vigorous exercise increases awareness and attention. Why might that be?

Awareness Inspiration

Role Models

J.R.R. Tolkien, author and myth maker, so deeply understood this world that he could create an unparalleled imaginary one complete with original languages. He believed that "fantasy remains a human right" for adults as well as children.

Isabel Allende, author whose prose and poetry weaves the spirituality of the Latin American culture through her stories of human search.

Alexander Calder, inventor of the mobile in 1930, was able to re-frame the present use of space and materials and visualize them floating in three dimensions.

Books and Movies For Younger People

Round Trip, Ann Jonas — an unsual picture book that demonstrates looking from a new point of view.

Jacques Cousteau's video series — exploring the undersea frontiers.

The Faithful Elephants, Yukio Tsuchiya— elephants in Tokyo's zoo are tragic victims of World War II.

Books and Movies For Older People

Hey World, Here I Am, Jean Little — poignant, insightful, smiling, thinking; a collection of poems about a girl growing up which helps us see life in a new light.

Cry the Beloved Country, Alan Paton — a man of power and a man of peace form an unlikely union and find understanding that could heal a nation.

Destiny's Road, Larry Niven — Jemmy grows up in a world far away and dreams of understanding the past. When an accident drives him from his parents' farm, he must overcome barriers of habit and ignorance.

Trader, Charles de Lint — discovering the responsibilities of privilege, Max is torn from his complacent life as a luthier (lute maker) into a world of dangerous magic. He must discover purpose or lose himself.

Emotional
Intelligence

Courage

Adversity

Perseverance

Interdependence

Empathy

Creativity

Noble Goal

Motivation

Curiosity

Accountability

Optimism

Forgiveness

Initiative

Conflict

Humor

Tolerance

Service

Truth

Tranquility

Awareness

Resiliency

Self-Control

Fusion

Integrity

Resiliency

Resiliency is the pattern that lets us "bounce back" and try again. It comes from an abiding belief in the value of solving problems and meeting goals.

Resiliency is like the active part of optimism — it is taking the "we can work it out" feeling and turning it into new attempts, new strategies, and new efforts.

In science, "resiliency" means the power of a substance to return to its original form after being twisted, stretched, or manipulated. In EQ terms, not only does resiliency help us return to our original forms, but with added knowledge, skills, and stamina. Resiliency is not just survival — it is fueled by a commitment to growth, to the future, and to goodness.

Resiliency Activities

• Next time you feel like you have failed or are being crushed, imagine that the situation is a test. What attribute or strength of yours is being tested? What actions or beliefs do you need to pass the test?

• Make a collage of all the "bad stuff" that is happening. Then, each day, paste a positive picture covering part of the collage — and for that day, practice the quality shown in the positive picture.

• Resiliency requires collaborative action. Identify three goals, then list five people who want to help you reach each goal. Then, in difficult times, contact your collaborators.

• Make a storybook in which the hero/ine has strengths and qualities similar to yours.

• Often we seek to escape from adversity through passive activities like watching television or sleeping — overused, these lead to "dry rot" and sap your strength. Instead, divert your energy in a positive direction by participating in active tasks or with active groups. Fix the fence, paint the hallway, join a club, or volunteer at the hospital.

• Think of any habit you have not changed for "a long time" (10 years if you're over 40, 10 weeks if you are under 10). Deliberately change your method of accomplishing that task — take a new route — and practice flexibility.

• Build a relationship with someone who you see as a model of positive risk-taking — someone courageous. Write or call them frequently for a boost of optimism.

• Create a device to hold an egg so you can drop it 10' without the egg breaking. Draw or paint a device that would protect you in a similar manner. How would that device make you feel?

• On a note card, write something negative or frustrating about your situation or surroundings. Then, carry the card all day, every day, until you can write five positive aspects of that negative. Ask people for their ideas. Once you have five positives, you can put the card away and make a new one.

Emotional Intelligence / Courage / Adversity / Perseverance / Interdependence / Empathy / Creativity / Noble Goal / Motivation / Curiosity / Accountability / Optimism / Forgiveness / Initiative / Conflict / Humor / Tolerance / Service / Truth / Tranquility / Awareness / **Resiliency** / Self-Control / Fusion / Integrity

Resiliency Quotes

"I seldom think about my limitations, and they never make me sad. Perhaps there is just a touch of yearning at times; but it is vague, like a breeze among flowers."

— Helen Keller

"If you want the rainbow, you gotta put up with the rain."

— Dolly Parton

"Fall seven times, stand up eight".

— Japanese proverb

Research Says...

Resilient individuals can block out the negativity of their surroundings/environment. Instead, they see opportunities in obstacles; they believe stumbling blocks are stepping stones; they recognize that frustration can be a force to teach new skills; that problems are places to try more creative strategies.

Resiliency Fusion Questions

How much "bounce back" did you demonstrate in your last challenge? Did you come back with more knowledge or skill — or did you just make it through?

If you could change one aspect of your personality to make yourself more resilient, what would you change?

Do all people have the same source of resiliency? What is/are the source(s)?

Iron is strong, but it is not resilient (it stays bent) — so what personality characteristics are like iron? What natural material is a metaphor for your personality?

Do you think babies are naturally resilient, or do they learn that skill? What evidence do you have?

How do you know if someone has the "bounce back plus" explained on the previous page? In what ways do they act differently?

Resiliency Inspiration

Emotional
Intelligence

Courage

Adversity

Perseverance

Interdependence

Empathy

Creativity

Noble Goal

Motivation

Curiosity

Accountability

Optimism

Forgiveness

Initiative

Conflict

Humor

Tolerance

Service

Truth

Tranquility

Awareness

Resiliency

Self-Control

Fusion

Integrity

Role Models

Corizone Aquino became president of the Philippines after Marcos fled.

Rabbi Harold Schulweis founded the Jewish Foundation for Christian Rescuers.

Rigoberta Menchu, a Guatemalan Indian, became spokesperson for indigenous peoples throughout the Americas and won the Nobel Peace Prize in 1992.

Books and Movies For Younger People

Amazing Grace, Mary Hoffman — a young girl follows her dreams despite labels some classmates try to put on her.

It's Going to Be Perfect!, Nancy Carlson — a new mother's expectations are dashed by reality; her optimistic attitude redefines "perfect" as the way things are, rather than the way she imagined they would be.

Thank You, Mr. Falker, Patricia Polacco — with the help of a sensitive teacher, a girl learns to read in spite of dyslexia.

My Big Sister Takes Drugs, Judith Vigna — a family struggles with difficult decisions.

Oliver — In Disney's adaptation of the Dickens novel, a kitten finds strength from friends and from heart.

Books and Movies For Older People

Nectar in a Sieve, Kamala Markandaya — a woman fights to keep her family together despite poverty and illness.

Avalon — the story of an immigrant family's rise from poverty to prosperity accomplished through humor and abiding love.

Parable of the Sower, Octavia Butler — engineered as an empath, Lauren becomes a beacon to the oppressed and disenfranchised. She is the harbinger of change.

Smila's Sense of Snow — in the face of pressure and betrayal, a young woman goes to the ends of the earth to learn why her young friend was killed.

Self-Control

"What it lies in our power to do,
it lies in our power not to do."
— Aristotle

We want chocolate <u>now</u>, we are hurt and we want revenge, we are scared and we want to hide. This is normal and not unusual. It is also healthy and useful to redirect these impulses.

For instance, when we are sad and want to break down crying, there is nothing wrong with the feeling. Doing so might help. But then we still have to resolve the situation that made us sad. Effective self-control lets us pause, reflect, and then use energy generated by the feeling to recognize and solve the underlying problem.

Sadly, many people think "self-control" means "do not feel." Instead it means act with clarity and intention.

The importance of mastery — of creating a life of balance — has been an issue as long as people have walked the earth. When we are dominated by a passion — for food, friends, power, sex — it leads to arrogance and megalomania. The extremes undermine our stability and reduce our effectiveness.

Self-Control Activities

• Reinforcement is critical to building new patterns; when you practice a self-control technique, acknowledge your efforts.

• Make an appointment with yourself — don't break it! Use the opportunity to scrutinize your actions, beliefs, decisions, etc. What needs improvement? Set a goal for the month, and include how you will celebrate your progress.

• Think of five recent events (e.g., test at school, project at work or home, social activity). Imagine what would have happened if you had planned your time so that you had more time for each of these. How would the outcome have changed?

• For your next project or task, create an analysis chart with three columns: "Questions," "Predictions," and "Evidence." Generate six critical questions, make predictions, and as you work on the project, note evidence. When you are through, reflect on how anticipating major questions changed the outcome of the project.

• For one month, practice the first Six Seconds rule: Pause for six seconds before responding. Keep track of how many times you use the technique. At the end of the month, discuss the experiment with family, friends, classmates, or co-workers.

• One of the best ways to strengthen self-control is to make and keep promises — they can be to yourself or to others. For example, "I will get up five minutes earlier every day this week," or "I will meet you for a walk in the park every Wednesday this month."

• Create a rubric to assess self-control, where 1 = impulsive and 5 = careful (your rubric should have more detail). As you read stories or discuss real or fictional characters, assess them with the rubric. Then, start the habit of self-assessment ("Oops, I shouldn't have raised my voice, that was a '2.'")

• Make an illustrated flow chart that shows what happens when self-control is not used. Start with a drawing or magazine picture that illustrates someone losing self-control, then connect it to another that shows the result, and continue the cycle.

Emotional
Intelligence
Courage
Adversity
Perseverance
Interdependence
Empathy
Creativity
Noble Goal
Motivation
Curiosity
Accountability
Optimism
Forgiveness
Initiative
Conflict
Humor
Tolerance
Service
Truth
Tranquility
Awareness
Resiliency
Self-Control
Fusion
Integrity

Self-Control Quotes

You cannot dream yourself into a character; you must hammer and forge yourself one.

— James A. Froude

"Nothing is more difficult, and therefore more precious, than to be able to decide."
— Napolean Bonaparte

"Wise time management is really the wise management of ourselves."
— Spencer W. Kimball

Research Says...

The ability to postpone gratification is essential to academic, emotional, or social success. The famous marshmellow test (i.e., Walter Mischel's study at Bing Nursury School) demonstrates that age-appropriate abilities to delay the immediate satisfaction of desires build problem-solving skills that support long-term goals. Those who can resist the moment become more socially competent, more personally effective, more self-assertive, and better able to cope with life's frustrations.

Self-Control Fusion Questions

Some people feel "out of control" and want life to be different. What can they change? Are there some parts of yourself that should not be under your control — why or why not?

If you were arrested for failure to show enough kindness, would there be enough evidence to free you?

Who are you becoming?

What is the difference between "self-control" and being "controlling"?

How do you know when self-control is too extreme and turns into "repression"?

Self-Control Inspiration

Role Models

Jack LaLanne — harbinger of the modern fitness movement, created first tv show, first weight machines, weight lifting for women, and continues to lead by example in his eighties with physical feats each birthday.

Morihei Ueshiba O'Sensei — founder of Aikido, a martial art based on redirecting energy through self-control, said, "Depending on the circumstance, you should be hard as a diamond, flexible as a willow, smooth-flowing like water, or as empty as space."

Books and Movies For Younger People

Stanley and Rhoda, Rosemary Wells — a boy has to learn to control his anger at his sibling.

My Little Sister Ate One Hare, Bill Grossman — greed can become an unhealthy habit with "distasteful" consequences.

Fritz and The Mess Fairy, Rosemary Wells — a taste of his own medicine reminds Fritz to clean up his act.

Popcorn Days and Buttermilk Nights, Gary Paulsen — a boy who has trouble with the law finds strength and purpose when he becomes part of a rural community.

The Empire Strikes Back — in the second episode of the epic, young Luke must learn to master his actions, his fears, and his beliefs.

Books and Movies For Older People

I Hadn't Meant to Tell You This, Jacqueline Woodsen — an abused girl must decide how to both take care of herself and protect her sisters.

Imperfect Control, Judith Viorst — our lifelong conflict between power and surrender reveals how sense of self and interpersonal relationships are colored by our struggle over control.

Good Will Hunting — a brilliant but underachieving youth struggles to reconcile his past, his dreams, and his daily actions.

Emotional
Intelligence

Courage

Adversity

Perseverance

Interdependence

Empathy

Creativity

Noble Goal

Motivation

Curiosity

Accountability

Optimism

Forgiveness

Initiative

Conflict

Humor

Tolerance

Service

Truth

Tranquility

Awareness

Resiliency

Self-Control

Fusion

Integrity

You have one brain. You have one self. You have one identity. Yet in our daily lives we divide ourselves up. Our life-with-family gets separated from our work; our emotions get separated from our cognition. So imagine putting it all back together, all going the same place at the same time.

Fusion is putting all the different parts of your brain and identity together. It melds your greatest attributes (i.e., personal, psychological, intellectual, ethical, creative...). Fusion occurs when you combine cognitive (thinking), emotional, and creative energies. The result: an intense burst of energy, power, efficacy, and a total absorption into your task or project.

To encourage fusion, use your EQ skills to create communication, trust, self-awareness, and purpose. Create an environment that stimulates heart and mind. The fusion questions in the book, for example, are designed to stimulate both emotional and cognitive intelligences. Finally, make sure that levels of skills and challenges match — tasks that are too hard generate frustration, too easy generate boredom. When people are caring, stretching, growing, and accomplishing they are ready for fusion.

Fusion

Fusion Activities

- Frequently and randomly — at least five times a day — check in with yourself. How is your energy? Level of focus/productivity? Emotional state? Who is with you? Do you wish you were doing something else? Are you in "flow" (that creative state where you are fully absorbed)? In fusion? By monitoring in this manner, you can teach yourself to create a more optimal set of circumstances.

- Fusion requires the confluence of passion and intellect — so you need ideas that you *care about* and cares about which you can *think*. Seek leisure activities that stimulate rather than pacify. For example, when you "veg out" in front of the tv, switch to PBS or The Discovery Channel.

- Reading is a more active form of entertainment than tv or movies — reading requires more parts of your brain. So make reading a habit.

- Friendship is a powerful force to promote fusion. A group of people who are excited about an idea helps create an environment that makes the brain most productive. This month, set a goal of creating one new friendship. Send Six Seconds a postcard about what happens.

- If you were going to create an ideal museum, what would it include? Design either the whole museum or just one exhibit. Make sure it promotes fusion!

- Do you know someone who inspires a combination of passion and intellectual curiosity? Observe that person and see if you can identify three actions, phrases, attitudes, tones of voice, or other qualities that are inspiring. Try using them!

- Create an imaginary world or environment. How would people treat one another? What would children learn? How would adults and children work together?

- Paint a picture of your feelings. Label them with words — what do the different feelings mean?

- Make a mobile where thoughts, feelings, and actions each have unique color. Can you design it so the mobile reflects your personal values, feelings, and identity?

Emotional
Intelligence
Courage
Adversity
Perseverance
Interdependence
Empathy
Creativity
Noble Goal
Motivation
Curiosity
Accountability
Optimism
Forgiveness
Initiative
Conflict
Humor
Tolerance
Service
Truth
Tranquility
Awareness
Resiliency
Self-Control
Fusion
Integrity

Fusion Quotes

"I change myself, I change the world."   — Gloria Anzaldua

"If you don't like the way the world is, you change it. You have an obligation to change it. You just do it one step at a time."
    — Marian Wright Edelman

"Dreams come in a size too big so that we can grow into them."
    — Josie Bisset

"The creation of a thousand forests is in one acorn."
    — Ralph Waldo Emerson

"When love and skill work together expect a masterpiece."
    — John Ruskin

Research Says...

Approximately one in five people report that they have had a feeling of being so absorbed in an activity that nothing else matters and that time ceases to exist.

Fusion Questions

What makes you most effective?

Why do people usually separate feelings and ideas?

What is the most fulfilling use of your time? Do you think most people would feel the same way as you?

Fusion Inspiration

Role Models

Thomas Adeoye Lambo, African psychiatrist, fused African and Western medicines in discovering the benefits of tribal/familial bonds in treating mental illness.

Paul Robeson — a "renaissance man" of unwavering ideals; one of the first African American singers/actors to win worldwide recognition. He was an outspoken critic of racial injustice and oppression of the poor.

Frank Lloyd Wright — American architect whose designs were based on natural forms and who created total living/working environments.

Books and Movies For Younger People

Cows Can't Fly, David Milgrim — or can they? A young artist's fertile imagination challenges the wisdom of the day.

Seven Blind Mice, Ed Young — knowing in part may make a fine tale, but wisdom comes from seeing the whole.

Mulan — to save her family, a young woman must discover new strengths and inner resources.

Books and Movies For Older People

The Tao of Pooh, Benjamin Hoff — that effortlessly calm, reflective bear shows the way to wisdom.

The Color of Water, James McBride — a biracial man discovers identity, family, and the strength to excel in life without being a victim.

Hero With a Thousand Faces, Joseph Campbell — a hero's journey fuses myth, dreams, and art.

IQ — to win the love of Einstein's niece, a young car mechanic must discover untapped capabilities.

36 Views of Mt. Fuji, Cathy Davidson — a compelling portrait of Japan, of being a woman, and of connections between people.

Emotional Intelligence

Courage

Adversity

Perseverance

Interdependence

Empathy

Creativity

Noble Goal

Motivation

Curiosity

Accountability

Optimism

Forgiveness

Initiative

Conflict

Humor

Tolerance

Service

Truth

Tranquility

Awareness

Resiliency

Self-Control

Fusion

Integrity

Integrity

"We become what we do."
— Chiang Kai-S

Integrity essentially means integrating principles, values, and actions. It allows us to take the harder path. Even when we would like to give in, when we would prefer to simply accept another's truth, integrity compels us to action.

To achieve integrity, we must balance the disparate forces that exist within and around us. It involves synthesizing these influences and then setting priorities to shape our daily lives.

Most importantly, integrity comes from compassionate and caring action based on deeply held beliefs. Moral/ethical character is developed from the nexus of justice and mercy. Hear everyone's good advice, work hard to gather divergent viewpoints, and then listen carefully to your own self. Integrity is the first step to all goodness.

Integrity Activities

• Label a shoe box "Lost and Found Dreams." Whenever you dream or imagine a better self or a better world, put a note in the box. Visit your box monthly to check on your progress.

• Next holiday when you give gifts, identify five people to whom you ordinarily give material presents. What gift of the spirit (e.g., patience, harmony, or creativity) could you give this year? How can you wrap this present? What gift of spirit would you like to receive?

• Because integrity is so tied to acting on principle, you need to be clear about your principles. If you had to chose only five rules to guide your life, what would you choose? Make a plaque, a poster, or a t-shirt.

• Role play discussing a problem; but have each "actor" play a different member of the group. What did you learn by seeing some-one play you?

• Sometimes we need to dramatically remind ourselves that it is okay to change and grow. To do so, "confess" any negative habits and behaviors onto paper, burn the papers, and raise the phoenix. To remind yourself of your new focus, write a permission slip.

• Create a "trophy case" where examples of integrity from your class, family, or team are exhibited. Make 3x5 cards available, and invite anyone to post positive examples about others.

• With collage, drawing, and/or painting, make a picture of your hero-self. Put the picture someplace prominent, and each day, set a new goal to move you closer to your hero-self. You might also give him/her a name, and learn to hear her/his voice.

• Make a yearly ritual of looking over old appointment books, letters, and reviewing your past performance in integrity. Have you kept your promises to others? To yourself? How would you rate your integrity? What one area will you work on? What one area can you celebrate?

• Find attractive clear containers and have each person in the family/group make a promise jar. Each person should put an object (a beautiful shell, a rock, a feather, figurine) in her/his jar whenever s/he acts with integrity. The object should symbolize the act of integrity.

Emotional
Intelligence
Courage
Adversity
Perseverance
Interdependence
Empathy
Creativity
Noble Goal
Motivation
Curiosity
Accountability
Optimism
Forgiveness
Initiative
Conflict
Humor
Tolerance
Service
Truth
Tranquility
Awareness
Resiliency
Self-Control
Fusion
Integrity

Integrity Quotes

"Not hammer strokes, but dance of the water sings the pebbles into perfection."

— Rabindranath Tagore

"We make our habits — then our habits make us."   — anon

"It is easy to say 'no' when there is a deeper 'yes' burning inside."

— Stephen Covey

"The greatest way to live with honor in the world is to be what we pretend to be."   — Socrates

Research Says...

Cynicism expects the worst and has a toxic effect on the body, while trust — a by-product of integrity — expects better and has a nontoxic effect. This physical result has been demonstrated many times; in one study, secular Jews had four times the rate of heart disease as temple-going Jews.

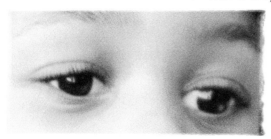

Spirituality encourages health-building integrity, so if you are not religious, make sure you get your daily dose of integrity another way.

Integrity Fusion Questions

Which integrity is more important — commitments to yourself or commitments to others?

Do you expect more of others or more of yourself? What would happen if most people did what you do in this regard?

Are "white lies" breaches of integrity? Why/why not?

What keeps you from becoming the person you would like to be?

Many people say that integrity is handed down through the generations — why might that happen? Do you have an "elder" who has taught you right from wrong?

What is the difference between integrity for a group and integrity for an individual?

Integrity Inspiration

Role Models

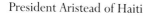

US Senator Barry Goldwater spoke his beliefs and maintained integrity.

Chief Seattle — in spite of overwhelming forces, he lived in accord with his principles and spoke them with clarity and strength.

President Aristead of Haiti — exiled by a military regime, he held faith with his people and the values of democracy, and was finally reinstated.

Books and Movies For Younger People

The Tent, Gary Paulsen — a crooked father becomes an evangelist to make money, but eventually finds faith.

The Pigs' Picnic, Keiko Kasza — a reminder that being ourselves is the most rewarding.

Finding Buck McHenry, Alfred Slote — when a grandpa volunteers to coach the Little League team, everyone learns from a former baseball great who is a role model of integrity.

Ordinary Magic by Malcolm Bosse — an orphaned boy transplanted from East India remains true to his beliefs despite social pressure to conform in America.

Books and Movies For Older People

The Long Walk Home — a black housekeeper walks miles each day to honor the Alabama bus boycott and wins the respect of her employer. Together they find common ground in a black and white world.

Midshipman's Hope, David Feintuch — compelled by an iron sense of duty, a young man finds himself commanding a spaceship and forced to make difficult decisions.

Emotional Intelligence
Courage
Adversity
Perseverance
Interdependence
Empathy
Creativity
Noble Goal
Motivation
Curiosity
Accountability
Optimism
Forgiveness
Initiative
Conflict
Humor
Tolerance
Service
Truth
Tranquility
Awareness
Resiliency
Self-Control
Fusion
Integrity